TORAH STUDIES

Printed in Canada, 2018

© Published and Copyrighted by
The Rohr Jewish Learning Institute
822 Eastern Parkway, Brooklyn, NY 11213

(888) YOUR-JLI / (718) 221-6900

www.myJLI.com

JEWISH LEARNING INSTITUTE

ב"ה

Torah Studies

Season Four 5778

Student Textbook

The ROHR JEWISH LEARNING INSTITUTE
gratefully acknowledges
the pioneering support of

George & Pamela
Rohr

Since its inception,
the JLI has been
a beneficiary of the vision,
generosity, care, and concern
of the Rohr family.

In the merit of
the tens of thousands of hours
of Torah study
by JLI students worldwide,
may they be blessed with health,
Yiddishe nachas from all their loved ones,
and extraordinary success
in all their endeavors.

DEDICATED TO

Mr. Yair Shamir

*With deep appreciation for his partnership
with JLI and leadership in bringing Torah
study to all corners of the world.*

*May he go from strength to strength and
enjoy health, happiness, nachat from his loved
ones, and success in all his endeavors.*

לאורך ימים ושנים טובות.

Contents

Love What You Do

Finding Pleasure in Purpose

*Dedicated by **Rabbi Mordechai** & **Esty Groner** in honor of their son, **Moshe Zeev's**, Bar Mitzvah—**23 Tamuz, 5778,** and in honor of the participants in the weekly Torah Studies class — Calgary, Alberta.*

PARSHAH OVERVIEW
Pinchas

Aaron's grandson Pinchas is rewarded for his act of zealotry in killing the Simeonite prince Zimri and the Midianite princess who was his paramour: G-d grants him a covenant of peace and the priesthood.

A census of the people counts 601,730 men between the ages of twenty and sixty. Moses is instructed on how the Land is to be divided by lottery among the tribes and families of Israel. The five daughters of Tzelafchad petition Moses that they be granted the portion of the Land belonging to their father, who died without sons; G-d accepts their claim and incorporates it into the Torah's laws of inheritance.

Moses empowers Joshua to succeed him and lead the people into the Land of Israel.

The Parshah concludes with a detailed list of the daily offerings, and the additional offerings brought on Shabbat, Rosh Chodesh (first of the month), and the festivals of Passover, Shavuot, Rosh Hashanah, Yom Kippur, Sukkot, and Shemini Atzeret.

Distributing
the Land

Equitable Portions

TEXT 1A

Bamidbar (Numbers) 26: 52–56

וַיְדַבֵּר ה׳ אֶל מֹשֶׁה לֵּאמֹר:

לָאֵלֶּה תֵּחָלֵק הָאָרֶץ בְּנַחֲלָה בְּמִסְפַּר שֵׁמוֹת:

לָרַב תַּרְבֶּה נַחֲלָתוֹ וְלַמְעַט תַּמְעִיט נַחֲלָתוֹ אִישׁ לְפִי פְקֻדָיו יֻתַּן נַחֲלָתוֹ:

אַךְ בְּגוֹרָל יֵחָלֵק אֶת הָאָרֶץ לִשְׁמוֹת מַטּוֹת אֲבֹתָם יִנְחָלוּ:

עַל פִּי הַגּוֹרָל תֵּחָלֵק נַחֲלָתוֹ בֵּין רַב לִמְעָט:

G-d spoke to Moses, saying:

You shall apportion the Land among these as an inheritance, in accordance with the number of names.

To the large [tribe] you shall give a larger inheritance and to a smaller tribe you shall give a smaller inheritance; each person shall be given an inheritance according to his [family] size.

Only through lottery shall the Land be apportioned; they shall inherit it according to the names of their fathers' tribes.

The inheritance shall be apportioned between the numerous and the few, according to the lot.

TEXT 1B

Rashi, Numbers 26:52

לְרַב תַּרְבֶּה נַחֲלָתוֹ: לְשֵׁבֶט שֶׁהָיָה מְרוּבֶּה בָּאוּכְלוּסִין נָתְנוּ חֵלֶק רַב,
וְאַף עַל פִּי שֶׁלֹּא הָיוּ הַחֲלָקִים שָׁוִים, שֶׁהֲרֵי הַכֹּל לְפִי רִבּוּי הַשֵּׁבֶט
חָלְקוּ הַחֲלָקִים . . .
וְלֹא נִתְחַלְּקָה הָאָרֶץ בְּמִדָּה, לְפִי שֶׁיֵּשׁ גְּבוּל מְשׁוּבָּח מֵחֲבֵרוֹ, אֶלָּא
בְּשׁוּמָא: בֵּית כּוֹר רַע כְּנֶגֶד בֵּית סְאָה טוֹב. הַכֹּל לְפִי הַדָּמִים.

Rabbi Shlomo Yitzchaki (Rashi)
1040–1105

Most noted biblical and Talmudic commentator. Born in Troyes, France, Rashi studied in the famed *yeshivot* of Mainz and Worms. His commentaries on the Pentateuch and the Talmud, which focus on the straightforward meaning of the text, appear in virtually every edition of the Talmud and Bible.

"To the large you shall give a large inheritance." To the tribe with a large population you shall allocate a larger portion. The portions were unequal since the portions were divided according to the size of the tribes. . . .

The Land was not divided solely according to measurements, because some areas were superior to others. Rather, it was assessed as follows: an inferior piece of land sufficient to sow a kor [an ancient measurement] was equivalent to a superior piece sufficient to sow a se'ah [a thirtieth of a kor]. It all depended on the value of the soil.

The Prophetic Lottery

TEXT 1C

Rashi, ibid.

לא עשו אלא על ידי גורל, והגורל היה על פי רוח הקודש, כמו
שמפורש בבבא בתרא אלעזר הכהן היה מלובש באורים ותומים,
ואומר ברוח הקדש אם שבט פלוני עולה, תחום פלוני עולה עמו.
והשבטים היו כתובים בי"ב פתקין, וי"ב גבולים בי"ב פתקין, ובללום
בקלפי והנשיא מכניס ידו לתוכה ונוטל שני פתקין. עולה בידו פתק
של שם שבטו, ופתק של גבול המפורש לו.

*The portions were decided by lot, and the lot was
determined by the Divine Spirit, as the Talmud clearly
states, "Elazar the Kohen was clad with the* Urim and
Tumim *(the breastplate that held a parchment with
the inscription of the Divine ineffable name), and he
said, while inspired by the Divine Spirit, "If such-and-
such a tribe is drawn, then such-and-such a territory
will be allocated to it."*

*The names of the tribes were inscribed on twelve slips
of paper, and the twelve territories were inscribed on
twelve other slips. The two sets of paper were mixed
together in a box and the tribe chieftain placed his hand
in the box and drew out two slips. His hand brought
up one slip bearing the name of his tribe and another
slip bearing the name of the territory designated for
his tribe.*

The Excluded Tribe

TEXT 2

Maimonides, Mishneh Torah, Negative Commandments #169

שלא יקח כל שבט לוי חלק בארץ, שנאמר "ונחלה לא יהיה לו"
(דברים יח:ב).

T he tribe of Levi should take no portion of the L and of Israel, as it is stated, "He shall not receive an inheritance."

Rabbi Moshe ben Maimon
(Maimonides, Rambam)
1135–1204

Halachist, philosopher, author, and physician. Maimonides was born in Córdoba, Spain. After the conquest of Córdoba by the Almohads, he fled Spain and eventually settled in Cairo, Egypt. There, he became the leader of the Jewish community and served as court physician to the vizier of Egypt. He is most noted for authoring the *Mishneh Torah*, an encyclopedic arrangement of Jewish law, and for his philosophical work, *Guide for the Perplexed*. His rulings on Jewish law are integral to the formation of halachic consensus.

TEXT 3

Talmud Tractate Bava Batra, 122a

עתידה ארץ ישראל שתתחלק לשלשה עשר שבטים, שבתחלה
לא נתחלקה אלא לשנים עשר שבטים.

When the Messiah comes, Israel is destined to be allocated to thirteen tribes, whereas in the first division, it was only allocated to twelve tribes.

Babylonian Talmud

A literary work of monumental proportions that draws upon the legal, spiritual, intellectual, ethical, and historical traditions of Judaism. The 37 tractates of the Babylonian Talmud contain the teachings of the Jewish sages from the period after the destruction of the Second Temple through the fifth century CE. It has served as the primary vehicle for the transmission of the Oral Law and the education of Jews over the centuries; it is the entry point for all subsequent legal, ethical, and theological Jewish scholarship.

Eternality of a Mitzvah

TEXT 4A

Maimonides, Mishneh Torah, Laws of the Foundations of the Torah, 8:1

דבר ברור ומפורש בתורה שהיא מצוה עומדת לעולם ולעולמי
עולמים, אין לה לא שינוי, ולא גרעון, ולא תוספת, שנאמר "את
כל הדבר אשר אנכי מצוה אתכם, אותו תשמרון לעשות. לא תוסף
עליו ולא תגרע ממנו." ונאמר, "והנגלות לנו ולבנינו עד עולם לעשות
את כל דברי התורה הזאת." הא למדת, שכל דברי תורה מצווין אנו
לעשותן עד עולם.

*It is abundantly clear in the Torah that G-d's com-
mandment remains forever without change, addition,
or diminishment, as it is stated, "All these matters that
I command to you, you shall be careful to perform.
You may not add to it or diminish from it," and it is
similarly stated, "What is revealed is for us and our
children forever, to carry out all the words of this Torah." This teaches that we are commanded to fulfill all
the Torah's directives forever.*

TEXT 4B

Talmud Tractate Megilah, 2b

"אלה המצות"—שאין נביא רשאי לחדש דבר.

The verse states, "These are the Commandments." This teaches us that a prophet is not permitted to introduce novel changes to the Torah.

Expanding the Land

TEXT 5

Maimonides, Mishneh Torah, Laws of Shemitah and Yovel, 13:10

כל שבט לוי מוזהרין שלא ינחלו בארץ כנען, וכן הן מוזהרין שלא
יטלו חלק בביזה בשעה שכובשין את הערים, שנאמר, "לא יהיה
לכהנים הלוים כל שבט לוי חלק ונחלה עם ישראל."
"חלק" בביזה, ו"נחלה" בארץ.

The entire tribe of Levi is forbidden to receive an inheritance in the land of Canaan. They are similarly forbidden to receive a share in the spoils when cities are conquered, as it is stated, "The priest and the Levite— the entire tribe of Levi—should not have a portion and an inheritance among Israel."

The words "a portion" refer to a portion of the spoils. The words "an inheritance" refer to a portion of the land.

TEXT 6A

Bereishit (Genesis) 15:18–21

בַּיּוֹם הַהוּא כָּרַת ה' אֶת אַבְרָם בְּרִית לֵאמֹר לְזַרְעֲךָ נָתַתִּי אֶת הָאָרֶץ
הַזֹּאת מִנְּהַר מִצְרַיִם עַד הַנָּהָר הַגָּדֹל נְהַר פְּרָת:
אֶת הַקֵּינִי וְאֶת הַקְּנִזִּי וְאֵת הַקַּדְמֹנִי:
וְאֶת הַחִתִּי וְאֶת הַפְּרִזִּי וְאֶת הָרְפָאִים:
וְאֶת הָאֱמֹרִי וְאֶת הַכְּנַעֲנִי וְאֶת הַגִּרְגָּשִׁי וְאֶת הַיְבוּסִי:

On that day, G-d formed a covenant with Abram, say-ing, "To your seed I have given this land, from the river of Egypt until the great river, the Euphrates River.

"The Kenites, the Kenizites, and the Kadmonites.

"And the Hittites, and the Perizites, and the Rephaim.

"And the Amorites, and the Canaanites, and the Gir-gashites, and the Jebusites."

TEXT 6B

Rashi, ad loc.

עשר אומות יש כאן, ולא נתן להם אלא שבעה גוים. והשלשה,
אדום, ומואב, ועמון, והם קיני קניזי וקדמוני, עתידים להיות ירושה
לעתיד, שנאמר, "אדום ומואב משלוח ידם ובני עמון משמעתם."

There are ten nations enumerated here, but G-d gave
them only seven nations. The other three—Edom,
Moab, and Ammon, which are referred to here as the
Kenites, the Kenizites, and the Kadmonites—are destined to become our heritage in the future, as it is stated,
"Upon Edom and Moab shall they stretch forth their
hand, and the children of Ammon shall obey them."

TEXT 7

The Lubavitcher Rebbe, Likutei Sichot, vol. 38, p. 107

Rabbi Menachem Mendel Schneerson
1902–1994

The towering Jewish leader of the 20th century, known as "the Lubavitcher Rebbe," or simply as "the Rebbe." Born in southern Ukraine, the Rebbe escaped Nazi-occupied Europe, arriving in the U.S. in June 1941. The Rebbe inspired and guided the revival of traditional Judaism after the European devastation, impacting virtually every Jewish community the world over. The Rebbe often emphasized that the performance of just one additional good deed could usher in the era of Mashiach. The Rebbe's scholarly talks and writings have been printed in more than 200 volumes.

ובפשטות כוונתו ב"ארץ כנען," לשלול ארץ שבעצם היא שייכת לארץ ישראל אבל אינה מארץ כנען, והוא ארץ קיני, קניזי, וקדמוני. ועל פי זה מובן דגם לדעת הרמב"ם אפשר לאמר ולפרש הא ד"שער לוי אחד," דלעתיד יקחו חלק בארץ, אבל לא בארץ כנען אלא בארץ קיני, קניזי, וקדמוני. ואזהרה ד"לא יהי' לכהנים הלוים כל שבט לוי חלק ונחלה עם ישראל," היא מצוה הנוהגת לדורות בארץ כנען.

By using the name Canaan, Maimonides intends to exclude lands that belong to Israel but are not part of the land of Canaan. They are the lands of the Kenites, the Kenizites, and the Kadmonites.

Accordingly, we can suggest that according to Maimonides, the tribe of Levi will inherit a portion in the Land, but not in what was once the land of Canaan, only in the lands of Kenites, Kenizites, and Kadmonites.

And the commandment "The Levitic kohanim, *the entire tribe of Levi, shall have no portion or inheritance with Israel" applies eternally to the land of Canaan.*

Living Jewishly

Why Is the New Land Different?

TEXT 8

Maimonides, Mishneh Torah, Laws of Shemitah and Yovel, 13:12

ולמה לא זכה לוי בנחלת ארץ ישראל ובביזתה עם אחיו? מפני שהובדל לעבוד את השם, לשרתו, ולהורות דרכיו הישרים ומשפטיו הצדיקים לרבים, "שנאמר יורו משפטיך ליעקב ותורתך לישראל." לפיכך הובדלו מדרכי העולם. לא עורכין מלחמה כשאר ישראל, ולא נוחלין, ולא זוכין לעצמן בכח גופן. אלא הם חיל השם, שנאמר, "ברך השם חילו." והוא ברוך הוא זוכה להם, שנאמר, אני חלקך ונחלתך."

Why did the Levites not receive a portion in the inheritance of Israel and in the spoils of war like their brethren?

Because they were set aside to serve G-d and to teach His just paths and righteous judgments to the people, as it is written (Deuteronomy 33:10), "They will teach Your judgments to Jacob and Your Torah to Israel." Therefore, they were set apart from the ways of the world. They do not wage war like the remainder of the Jewish people, nor do they receive an inheritance, nor do they acquire for themselves through their physical power.

Instead, they are G-d's legion, as it is written, "G-d has blessed His legion." G-d also provides for them, as it is written, "I am your portion and your inheritance."

TEXT 9

The Lubavitcher Rebbe, Likutei Sichot, vol. 30, p. 250–251

Likutei Sichot
Widely considered the Rebbe's magnum opus, the 39 volumes of Likutei Sichot feature scholarly essays relating to themes in the weekly Torah portions and the Jewish holidays. The Rebbe initially conveyed these concepts in his public talks and subsequently reworked them for publication. In some volumes, the essays appear in Yiddish, while in others they are in Hebrew. Most volumes also present a collection of the Rebbe's correspondence.

תַּכְלִית עֲבוֹדָתָם שֶׁל בְּנֵי יִשְׂרָאֵל הִיא לַעֲשׂוֹת לוֹ יִתְבָּרֵךְ דִּירָה בַּתַּחְתּוֹנִים דַּוְקָא, שֶׁקְּדוּשָׁתוֹ יִתְבָּרֵךְ תִּשְׁרֶה בְּ"אַרְצִיּוּת" שֶׁל עוֹלָם הַזֶּה הַגַּשְׁמִי דַּוְקָא (שֶׁלָּכֵן רוֹב מִצְוֹת הַתּוֹרָה הֵן מִצְוֹת מַעֲשִׂיּוֹת, כְּדֵי שֶׁעַל יְדֵי קִיּוּם הַתּוֹרָה וּמִצְוֹת תּוּמְשַׁךְ קְדוּשָׁה (גַּם) בְּעִנְיָנִים הַגַּשְׁמִיִּים) ...

דַּוְקָא מִשּׁוּם זֶה נִיתְּנָה לוֹ אֶרֶץ יִשְׂרָאֵל, אֶרֶץ גַּשְׁמִית, שֶׁבָּה תְּלוּיוֹת כַּמָּה וְכַמָּה מִצְוֹת הַתּוֹרָה ... מֵאַחַר שֶׁזֶּהוּ עִנְיַן בְּנֵי יִשְׂרָאֵל וְהַתּוֹרָה – "לִכְבּוֹשׁ" אֶת הָ"אַרְצִיּוּת" שֶׁל עוֹלָם הַזֶּה וְלַעֲשׂוֹתוֹ דִּירָה לוֹ יִתְבָּרֵךְ.

The mission and purpose of the Jewish people is to turn the lowest reality into a home for G-d, namely that G-d should be expressed through the materiality of this physical world. (This is why most mitzvot are action-based—so that sanctity will be expressed in the physical realm as well.) . . .

For this reason, the Land of Israel was given to the Jewish people, a physical land where many of the mitzvot find their only expression . . . because the purpose of the Jewish people and the Torah is to conquer the materiality of this world and turn it into a home for G-d.

TEXT 10

The Lubavitcher Rebbe, Likutei Sichot, vol. 38, pp. 108

מה שישראל יקבלו לעתיד לבא ארץ קיני, קניזי, וקדמוני, אינה בסוג נחלה כמו ארץ כנען, ארץ ז' עממין שיש להם לישראל ארץ בעולם, אלא נתינה מיוחדת מאת השם. וכמו שכתוב, "ואם ירחיב השם אלקיך את גבולך"- לא מצד ההכרח דישובם בארץ. ואם כן שפיר יכולום הלויים לקבל בזה.

The lands of the Kenites, the Kenizites, and the Kad-monites that the Jews will inherit in the future is not the same kind of inheritance as the land of Canaan, the land of the seven nations. That land was given to Jews for the purpose of building a Jewish country in the world. This land will be a unique gift from G-d, as it is written (Deuteronomy 12:20), "When G-d will expand your boundaries." Therefore, the Levites will be able to inherit in this land.

Fusing Pleasure and Purpose

The Pursuit of Purpose

TEXT 11

"For Her Child's Future," Bronya Shaffer, www.chabad.org

My husband's first impression was of two children carrying a child. But when they came up the stairs, their faces dispelled any illusion of childishness. Married for several years, parents of six-year-old twins, their youngest child snuggled close within his father's parka.

. . . . When the twins were three, they celebrated the traditional haircut for their son, and the first Shabbat candlestick for their daughter—what a celebration that had been! She talked about her feeling of maternal Jewish continuity as she watched her little son, enveloped in his father's tallit, carried proudly into the local Jewish day school. Although not yet ready for school, he experienced his first taste of the sweetness of Torah study, and they cut their first tuition check.

But they couldn't afford that any longer. Precious as Jewish education is, they'd enrolled their children in the local public school. The cost was just too great, and in the economic crunch, sacrifices had to be made. . . .

I turned to look at my husband, and his eyes were on the little children. Then, softly, he faced the parents . . .

"Parents would sacrifice anything for their children," he said. *"What would a parent not do for a child's well-being? What wouldn't a parent give up for a child's future?" He touched the little boy's fist, and then turned to Jake: "He needs oxygen and food and water; he needs a Jewish education. It's not dispensable, it's not optional. It's his life, his future."*

Miriam stood up suddenly, as if to flee. Jake called her back, and brought her back to the chair beside him. "We can't do it," he said. "I know you think it's important, but we can't do it." And with that, thanking my husband and me, he stood to leave.

. . . But she sat, made no move. "Wait a minute," she said. "My father left me a college fund," she said to my husband. "He wasn't a wealthy man, but he willed to me a fund meant for my education through graduate school. Would it be unethical to use that fund for my children's education instead of mine?" she asked.

Jake stood frozen, but the warmth of her eyes now on him seemed to penetrate to some deep place. "You'd give that up?" he asked her. "Your security for enabling your dream? The untouchable fund that would allow you a graduate degree?"

And now she stood, gathering the blankets around her baby, wrapping him in her love, and then pressing his little body against his father's chest, zipping up his father's jacket around him. "Look around you," she said. "This is what our children need: a Jewish home to live in, and a Jewish environment to learn in."

Pulling on her coat and gloves, a long look around the room lined with holy books . . . and they were gone.

Finding Pleasure

TEXT 12

The Lubavitcher Rebbe, Likutei Sichot, vol. 4, p. 1216

רבי שמעון אומר: שלושה כתרים הם: כתר תורה וכתר כהונה וכתר מלכות. וכתר שם טוב עולה על גביהן.

דער ענין פון כתר מלכות איז קבלת עול מלכות שמים. וואס דאס איז די ערשטע פעולה וואס א איד דארף פועל'ן ביי זיך, ער זאל זיין גרייט צו דינען דעם אויבערשטען בכל מיני עבודת עבד. און אט דער קבלת עול איז זיין ערשטער פארבונד מיט אלוקות.

קבלת עול אליין איז אבער ניט מספיק. ווייל דער תכלית פון א אידן איז דאך אז ער זאל ווערען מיוחד מיטן אויבערשטען, און מצד קבלת עול אליין איז ער נאך אלץ א באזונדער מציאות. ואדרבה, ער איז אזא מציאות וואס ביי אים לייגען זיך ניט אפ די ציווויים פון אדון, און דער קיום רצון האדון איז ביי אים נאר בדרך קבלת עול. אויף דעם קומט שפעטער די עבודה פון כתר כהונה ביום הכיפורים, וואס דאן איז דער כהן גדול אריין "לפני ולפנים", אין דעם ארט וואו

עס געפֿינען זיך די לוחות, אויף וועלכע עס זײַנען געווען חקוק
די עשרת הדברות. די עשרת הדברות זײַנען ניט געווען **געשריבען**
אויף זיי, וואָס בײַ כתיבה איז דאַך דער דיו א דבר נוסף אויפֿן קלף,
נאָר זיי זײַנען געווען חקוק על הלוחות, "מני' ובי' ".
און בעבודת האדם מיינט עס אז ער פּועל'ט בײַ זיך דעם קישור
ויחוד מיט אלוקות, ניט נאָר בדרך קבלת עול, נאָר אז געטלעכקייט
ווערט זײַן "צורה"–זײַן געשמאַק, רצון וכו'.

"Rabbi Shimon would say: There are three crowns:
The crown of Torah, the crown of priesthood, and
the crown of kingship. But the crown of a good name
surpasses them all."

The crown of kingship refers to accepting G-d's reign—
the first step in establishing a bond with G-d. First and
foremost, a Jew must submit to G-d with the absolute
and total commitment of a subject toward his ruler.

Pledging fidelity to G-d and accepting G-d's kingship
is insufficient, for it implies the existence of a gap be-
tween subject and Ruler. This shortcoming is overcome
by the crown of priesthood, which enables a person to
develop an inner bond with G-d.

The crown of priesthood refers to the High Priest, who
entered the Holy of Holies, the place that held the Tab-
lets of the Ten Commandments. The Tablets represent
a perfect state of unity with G-d, for unlike written
letters, which remain separate from the parchment or

paper they are written on, the Ten Commandments were carved into the stone itself.

This represents those who develop a bond and oneness with G-d that transcends mere submission. Rather, their sole desire and pleasure is to fulfill the wish of G-d.

MATOT-MASSEI

The Perfect Orchestra

Nature's on Your Side

*Dedicated by **Rabbi Yosef Chaim Kantor** - Thailand*
In tribute to the great and important work of the Rohr Jewish Learning Institute

PARSHAH OVERVIEW
Matot-Massei

Moses conveys the laws governing the annulment of vows to the heads of the tribes of Israel. War is waged against Midian for their role in plotting the moral destruction of Israel, and the Torah gives a detailed account of the war spoils and how they were allocated amongst the people, the warriors, the Levites and the high priest.

The tribes of Reuben and Gad (later joined by half of the tribe of Manasseh) ask for the lands east of the Jordan as their portion in the Promised Land, these being prime pastureland for their cattle. Moses is initially angered by the request, but subsequently agrees on the condition that they first join, and lead, in Israel's conquest of the lands west of the Jordan.

The forty-two journeys and encampments of Israel are listed, from the Exodus to their encampment on the plains of Moab across the river from the land of Canaan. The boundaries of the Promised Land are given, and cities of refuge are designated as havens and places of exile for inadvertent murderers. The daughters of Tzelafchad marry within their own tribe of Manasseh, so that the estate which they inherit from their father should not pass to the province of another tribe

Taxes

The War on Midian

TEXT 1A

Bamidbar (Numbers) 31:1–2

וַיְדַבֵּר ה' אֶל מֹשֶׁה לֵּאמֹר:
נְקֹם נִקְמַת בְּנֵי יִשְׂרָאֵל מֵאֵת הַמִּדְיָנִים אַחַר תֵּאָסֵף אֶל עַמֶּיךָ:

G-d spoke to Moses saying,

"Take revenge for the children of Israel against the Midianites; afterwards you will be gathered to your people."

TEXT 1B

Ibid., v. 25–47

וַיֹּאמֶר ה' אֶל מֹשֶׁה לֵּאמֹר:
שָׂא אֵת רֹאשׁ מַלְקוֹחַ הַשְּׁבִי בָּאָדָם וּבַבְּהֵמָה אַתָּה וְאֶלְעָזָר הַכֹּהֵן וְרָאשֵׁי אֲבוֹת הָעֵדָה:
וְחָצִיתָ אֶת הַמַּלְקוֹחַ בֵּין תֹּפְשֵׂי הַמִּלְחָמָה הַיֹּצְאִים לַצָּבָא וּבֵין כָּל הָעֵדָה:
וַהֲרֵמֹתָ מֶכֶס לַה' מֵאֵת אַנְשֵׁי הַמִּלְחָמָה הַיֹּצְאִים לַצָּבָא אֶחָד נֶפֶשׁ מֵחֲמֵשׁ הַמֵּאוֹת מִן הָאָדָם וּמִן הַבָּקָר וּמִן הַחֲמֹרִים וּמִן הַצֹּאן:
מִמַּחֲצִיתָם תִּקָּחוּ וְנָתַתָּה לְאֶלְעָזָר הַכֹּהֵן תְּרוּמַת ה':

וּמִמַּחֲצַת בְּנֵי יִשְׂרָאֵל תִּקַּח אֶחָד אָחֻז מִן הַחֲמִשִּׁים מִן הָאָדָם מִן הַבָּקָר מִן הַחֲמֹרִים וּמִן הַצֹּאן מִכָּל הַבְּהֵמָה וְנָתַתָּה אֹתָם לַלְוִיִּם שֹׁמְרֵי מִשְׁמֶרֶת מִשְׁכַּן ה':

וַיַּעַשׂ מֹשֶׁה וְאֶלְעָזָר הַכֹּהֵן כַּאֲשֶׁר צִוָּה יְקֹוָק אֶת מֹשֶׁה:

וַיְהִי הַמַּלְקוֹחַ יֶתֶר הַבָּז אֲשֶׁר בָּזְזוּ עַם הַצָּבָא צֹאן שֵׁשׁ מֵאוֹת אֶלֶף וְשִׁבְעִים אֶלֶף וַחֲמֵשֶׁת אֲלָפִים:

וּבָקָר שְׁנַיִם וְשִׁבְעִים אָלֶף:

וַחֲמֹרִים אֶחָד וְשִׁשִּׁים אָלֶף:

וְנֶפֶשׁ אָדָם מִן הַנָּשִׁים אֲשֶׁר לֹא יָדְעוּ מִשְׁכַּב זָכָר כָּל נֶפֶשׁ שְׁנַיִם וּשְׁלֹשִׁים אָלֶף:

וַתְּהִי הַמֶּחֱצָה חֵלֶק הַיֹּצְאִים בַּצָּבָא מִסְפַּר הַצֹּאן שְׁלֹשׁ מֵאוֹת אֶלֶף וּשְׁלֹשִׁים אֶלֶף וְשִׁבְעַת אֲלָפִים וַחֲמֵשׁ מֵאוֹת:

וַיְהִי הַמֶּכֶס לַיקֹוָק מִן הַצֹּאן שֵׁשׁ מֵאוֹת חָמֵשׁ וְשִׁבְעִים:

וְהַבָּקָר שִׁשָּׁה וּשְׁלֹשִׁים אָלֶף וּמִכְסָם לַה' שְׁנַיִם וְשִׁבְעִים:

וַחֲמֹרִים שְׁלֹשִׁים אֶלֶף וַחֲמֵשׁ מֵאוֹת וּמִכְסָם לַה' אֶחָד וְשִׁשִּׁים:

וְנֶפֶשׁ אָדָם שִׁשָּׁה עָשָׂר אָלֶף וּמִכְסָם לַה' שְׁנַיִם וּשְׁלֹשִׁים נָפֶשׁ:

וַיִּתֵּן מֹשֶׁה אֶת מֶכֶס תְּרוּמַת ה' לְאֶלְעָזָר הַכֹּהֵן כַּאֲשֶׁר צִוָּה ה' אֶת מֹשֶׁה:

וּמִמַּחֲצִית בְּנֵי יִשְׂרָאֵל אֲשֶׁר חָצָה מֹשֶׁה מִן הָאֲנָשִׁים הַצֹּבְאִים:

וַתְּהִי מֶחֱצַת הָעֵדָה מִן הַצֹּאן שְׁלֹשׁ מֵאוֹת אֶלֶף וּשְׁלֹשִׁים אֶלֶף שִׁבְעַת אֲלָפִים וַחֲמֵשׁ מֵאוֹת:

וּבָקָר שִׁשָּׁה וּשְׁלֹשִׁים אָלֶף:

וַחֲמֹרִים שְׁלֹשִׁים אֶלֶף וַחֲמֵשׁ מֵאוֹת:

וְנֶפֶשׁ אָדָם שִׁשָּׁה עָשָׂר אָלֶף:

וַיִּקַּח מֹשֶׁה מִמַּחֲצִת בְּנֵי יִשְׂרָאֵל אֶת הָאָחֻז אֶחָד מִן הַחֲמִשִּׁים מִן הָאָדָם וּמִן הַבְּהֵמָה וַיִּתֵּן אֹתָם לַלְוִיִּם שֹׁמְרֵי מִשְׁמֶרֶת מִשְׁכַּן יְקֹוָק כַּאֲשֶׁר צִוָּה ה' אֶת מֹשֶׁה:

G-d spoke to Moses, saying,

"Take a count of the plunder of the captive people and animals, you, together with Eleazar the Kohen and the paternal leaders of the community.

"And you shall divide the plunder equally between the warriors who went out to battle and the entire congregation.

"And you shall levy a tax for G-d from the soldiers who went out to battle: one soul out of every five hundred, from the people, from the cattle, from the donkeys, and from the sheep.

"You shall take from their half and give it to Eleazar the Kohen as a gift to G-d.

"From the half belonging to the children of Israel you shall take one part out of fifty of the people, of the cattle, of the donkeys, of the sheep, and of all animals, and you shall give them to the Levites, the guardians of the Mishkan of G-d."

Moses and Eleazar the Kohen did as G-d had commanded Moses.

The plunder, which was in addition to the spoils that the army had spoiled, consisted of six hundred and seventy five thousand sheep.

Seventy two thousand cattle.

Sixty one thousand donkeys.

As for the people, of the women who had no experience of intimate relations with a man, all souls were thirty two thousand.

The half that was the portion of those who went out to battle: the number of sheep was three hundred and thirty seven thousand, five hundred.

The tax to G-d from the sheep was six hundred and seventy five.

Thirty six thousand cattle, of which the tax to G-d was seventy two.

Thirty thousand and five hundred donkeys, of which the tax to G-d was sixty one.

Sixteen thousand people, of which the tax to G-d was thirty two people.

Moses gave the tax which was a gift to G-d, to Eleazar the Kohen, as G-d had commanded Moses.

And from the half allotted to the children of Israel, which Moses had divided from the men who had gone into the army.

The community's half [consisted of] three hundred and thirty seven thousand, five hundred sheep.

Thirty six thousand cattle.

Thirty thousand five hundred donkeys.

And sixteen thousand people.

Moses took one part out of fifty from the half of the children of Israel, the people and the animals, and gave them to the Levites, the guardians of G-d's sanctuary as G-d commanded Moses.

	Sheep	Cows	Donkeys	People
Total	675,000	72,000	61,000	32,000
Soldiers	337,500	36,000	30,500	16,000
Tax	675	72	61	32
Given To	Eleazar	Eleazar	Eleazar	Eleazar
Civilians	337,500	36,000	30,500	16,000
Tax	6,750	720	610	320
Given To	Levites	Levites	Levites	Levites

Hearkening to Terumah

TEXT 2

Maimonides, Mishneh Torah, Laws of Terumah, 3:1–2

תרומה גדולה אין לה שיעור מן התורה, שנאמר ראשית דגנך כל
שהוא אפילו חטה אחת פוטרת הכרי, ולכתחלה לא יפריש אלא
כשיעור שנתנו חכמים ובזמן שהיא עומדת לשריפה מפני הטומאה
יש לו להפריש כל שהוא לכתחלה.

וכמה הוא שיעורה שנתנו חכמים, עין יפה אחד מארבעים, והבינונית
אחד מחמשים, רעה אחד מששים, ולא יפחות מאחד מששים.

Rabbi Moshe ben Maimon
(Maimonides, Rambam)
1135–1204

Halachist, philosopher, author, and physician. Maimonides was born in Córdoba, Spain. After the conquest of Córdoba by the Almohads, he fled Spain and eventually settled in Cairo, Egypt. There, he became the leader of the Jewish community and served as court physician to the vizier of Egypt. He is most noted for authoring the *Mishneh Torah*, an encyclopedic arrangement of Jewish law, and for his philosophical work, *Guide for the Perplexed*. His rulings on Jewish law are integral to the formation of halachic consensus.

There is no minimum requirement for terumah according to Scriptural Law, as [implied by the verse], "The first of your grain," i.e., even the slightest amount. Even one kernel of grain fulfills the requirement for the entire grain heap. As an initial and prefatory measure, one should separate only according to the measures specified by our Sages. In the present age, when [terumah] will be burnt because of impurity, a person may separate even the smallest amount as an initial and prefatory measure.

What is the measure that our Sages established? A generous measure is one fortieth [of the crop]. The average [measure] is one fiftieth and a parsimonious measure is one sixtieth.

TEXT 3

Maimonides, loc. cit

אין תורמין תרומה זו לא במדה ולא במשקל ולא במנין לפי שלא
נאמר בה שיעור אלא אומד ומפריש בדעתו כמו אחד מחמשים.

One should not separate this terumah *with a measure, a scale, or by number, because [the Torah] did not specify a measure for this [allocation]. Instead, one makes an estimation and separates one fiftieth according to his conception.*

TEXT 4

Rabbi Yosef Rosen, Tzafnat Pane'ach, Bamidbar, ad loc.

Rabbi Yosef Rosen
(Rogatchover Ga'on)
1858–1936
One of the prominent talmudic scholars of the early 20th century. Born in Rogachev, Belarus, to a Chasidic family, his unusual capabilities were recognized at a young age. At thirteen he was brought to Slutzk to study with Rabbi Yosef Ber Soloveitchik. He remained there for a full year, studying primarily with the rabbi's son, the legendary Chaim Soloveitchik. Later, he moved on to Shklov, where he studied with Rabbi Moshe Yehoshua Leib Diskin. After a period in Warsaw, the home city of his wife, he assumed the rabbinate of the Chasidic community in Dvinsk, Latvia. His works, titled *Tzafnat Pane'ach*, are famed for both their depth and difficulty.

הנה כאן לא מנה כמה הוה החלק שנתן ללוים, משום דהנה
בתוספתא תרומות . . . יליף מזה אסמכתא לשיעור תרומה [אחד
מנ'], והנה תרומה אסור במנין כמבואר במשנה שם ובכמה מקומות,
וזה נקט קרא אחוד רק אחוזה ולא מנה, ואתי שפיר כאן.

The Torah does not enumerate the amount that was actually paid to the Levites. The reason for this is because the Tosafot in Terumot... teach that our verses are the scriptural source for the notion that terumah *is one-fiftieth. Now,* terumah *is not allowed to be given exactly, as the Mishnah states clearly and in many other places. For this reason, Scripture states only the percentage and not the precise amount here.*

Miraculous Undertones

Frozen in Time

TEXT 5

Nachmanides, Pirush Haramban to Bamidbar ad loc.

Rabbi Moshe ben Nachman
(Nachmanides, Ramban)
1194–1270
Scholar, philosopher, author, and physician. Nachmanides was born in Spain and served as leader of Iberian Jewry. In 1263, he was summoned by King James of Aragon to a public disputation with Pablo Cristiani, a Jewish apostate. Though Nachmanides was the clear victor of the debate, he had to flee Spain because of the resulting persecution. He moved to Israel and helped reestablish communal life in Jerusalem. He authored a classic commentary on the Pentateuch and a commentary on the Talmud.

"ותהי המחצה חלק היצאים בצבא". הוצרך הכתוב לפרט הזה שיזכיר כמה המחצה וכמה המכס, להודיע כי מן היום שלקחו המלקוח הזה עד שמנו אותו וחצו אותו והפרישו ממנו המכס ונתנוהו לאלעזר הכהן מכל המקנה הגדול הזה לא מת אחד, וזה נס. וכן במחצת העדה ללוים.

"And from the half allotted to the children of Israel." Scripture deemed it necessary to mention exactly how much "half" amounted to as well as the precise amount of taxes to broadcast the following miracle: From the day the spoils were captured, until, and throughout, the entire time it was split, taxed, and ultimately given to Eleazar the High Priest, not a single member of this vast herd of cattle died. This is a great miracle.

The same miracle occurred with the half that was given to the civilian population and taxed to the Levites.

What's the Point?

TEXT 6

Nachmanides, Twelve Sermons, Sermon 8

שחפץ השם יתברך לקיים מנהגו של עולם בכל מה דאפשר,
ושהטבע יקר בעיניו לא ישנהו אלא לצורך הכרחי.

G-d wishes to maintain the status quo of the natural order as much as possible. Nature is dear to G-d, and He does not tamper with it if not absolutely necessary.

Perfect Math

TEXT 7

The Lubavitcher Rebbe, Likutei Sichot, vol. 13, p. 111

Likutei Sichot
Widely considered the Rebbe's magnum opus, the 39 volumes of Likutei Sichot feature scholarly essays relating to themes in the weekly Torah portions and the Jewish holidays. The Rebbe initially conveyed these concepts in his public talks and subsequently reworked them for publication. In some volumes, the essays appear in Yiddish, while in others they are in Hebrew. Most volumes also present a collection of the Rebbe's correspondence.

אם היה כתוב בתורה רק ציווי הקדוש ברוך הוא ולאחר זה "ויעש משה וגו'" ותו לא - מקום לשאלה גדולה ודוקא על פי פשטות העניינים: על פי טבע, בשבי ומלקוח כו' באדם ובבהמה לא שכיח הוא כלל וכלל אשר המספר דכל מין ומין בפני עצמו - יהיה מדוייק עד כדי כך שמחציתו של כל מין בפני עצמו יחולק לקבוצות של חמשים ושל חמש מאות, בלי שיוותר עודף! . . . ובמילא בנדון דידן, מכיון שהציווי היה ליקח מכס אחוז אחד מחמשים מחלק בני ישראל ואחד מחמש מאות מחלק אנשי הצבא, היה צריך להיות הוספה בהציווי מה לעשות בנוגע להעודף.

לכן מפרט הכתוב "ויהי המלקוח גו'" (כל המספרים בפרטיות)
להודיע שהיה בנדון דידן דיוק נפלא בכל מספרים אלו ודבכל מין
בפני עצמו היה מספר מדויק, באופן שלקחו אחד אחוז מחמשים
ואחד - מחמש מאות מהמחצית ולא היה עודף כלל.

Rabbi Menachem Mendel Schneerson
1902–1994

The towering Jewish leader of the 20th century, known as "the Lubavitcher Rebbe," or simply as "the Rebbe." Born in southern Ukraine, the Rebbe escaped Nazi-occupied Europe, arriving in the U.S. in June 1941. The Rebbe inspired and guided the revival of traditional Judaism after the European devastation, impacting virtually every Jewish community the world over. The Rebbe often emphasized that the performance of just one additional good deed could usher in the era of Mashiach. The Rebbe's scholarly talks and writings have been printed in more than 200 volumes.

If the Torah would have only recorded G-d's command and simply stated that "Moses carried it out…" with no further detail, a fundamental question in the basic narrative would have cropped up: Under normal circumstances, with such a large amount of human and livestock spoils, it's highly improbable that the number of each specific category would be so exact that when divided in half, it should equal exactly 50 or 500 without any remaining fraction.

Inasmuch as G-d levied a tax on the Jews in the amount of one 1/50th from the civilian population and one 1/500th from the soldiers, the Torah should have made it clear what they were to do with the remaining fractions [that didn't fit exactly into those numbers].

It is for this reason that Scripture enumerates everything in detail—to demonstrate that in this story, something remarkable happened: the numbers were so exact that the people were able to give their respective taxes of one 1/50th and one 1/500th without any remaining fraction!

A Perfect Orchestra

No Fractions

TEXT 8

Bamidbar (Numbers) 31:25–29

וַיֹּאמֶר ה' אֶל מֹשֶׁה לֵּאמֹר:

שָׂא אֵת רֹאשׁ מַלְקוֹחַ הַשְּׁבִי בָּאָדָם וּבַבְּהֵמָה אַתָּה וְאֶלְעָזָר הַכֹּהֵן וְרָאשֵׁי אֲבוֹת הָעֵדָה:

וְחָצִיתָ אֶת הַמַּלְקוֹחַ בֵּין תֹּפְשֵׂי הַמִּלְחָמָה הַיֹּצְאִים לַצָּבָא וּבֵין כָּל הָעֵדָה:

וַהֲרֵמֹתָ מֶכֶס לַה' מֵאֵת אַנְשֵׁי הַמִּלְחָמָה הַיֹּצְאִים לַצָּבָא אֶחָד נֶפֶשׁ מֵחֲמֵשׁ הַמֵּאוֹת מִן הָאָדָם וּמִן הַבָּקָר וּמִן הַחֲמֹרִים וּמִן הַצֹּאן:

מִמַּחֲצִיתָם תִּקָּחוּ וְנָתַתָּה לְאֶלְעָזָר הַכֹּהֵן תְּרוּמַת ה':

G-d spoke to Moses, saying,

"Take a count of the plunder of the captive people and animals, you, together with Eleazar the Kohen and the paternal leaders of the community.

And you shall divide the plunder equally between the warriors who went out to battle and the entire congregation.

And you shall levy a tax for G-d from the soldiers who went out to battle: one soul out of every five hundred, from the people, from the cattle, from the donkeys, and from the sheep.

You shall take from their half and give it to Eleazar the Kohen as a gift to G-d.

TEXT 9A

The Lubavitcher Rebbe, Likutei Sichot, vol 13, p. 112

והביאור בזה - בלשון הכתוב:

לאחרי הציווי "והרמת מכס לה' מאת אנשי המלחמה גו' אחד נפש מחמש המאות גו'" חוזר הכתוב ואומר "וממחציתם תקחו ונתתה גו'". מזה שהכתוב מדגיש "ממחציתם תקחו"—שלכאורה תיבות אלו מיותרות הן—מוכח שרצה הקדוש ברוך הוא שה"תקחו" דאחד מחמשים או דחמש מאות—יהיה מכל המחצית—ובאם היה עודף—הרי מאותו עודף לא הייתה כל קיחה!

The explanation lies in the words of the verse:

After G-d commanded the Jews, "And you shall levy a tax for G-d from the soldiers… one soul out of every five hundred, etc.," the verse repeats, "You shall take from their half. . . ." Now, these words are superfluous. From that fact that the verse stresses that the tax be taken "from their half," it is clear that the tax coming from the 50 or the 500 should come from the entire "half" [i.e., the entire portion received by that population (soldier or civilian)]. Should there be any remainder, that portion would not have been taxed!

Everything Part of the Mitzvah

TEXT 9B

Ibid.

וטעם הדבר בכדי שבני ישראל יוכלו לקיים ציווי הקדוש ברוך הוא,
שלזה צריך להיות מחצית בני ישראל בשוה למחצית אנשי הצבא
ושלא יהיה עודף . . .

*The reason for this entire matter was so that the
Jews would be able to fulfill G-d's command. Thus,
the amounts needed to be perfect—the civilian half
equal to that of the soldier's half without any remaining fractions.*

The Lesson

TEXT 9C

Ibid.

ההוראה מענין הנ"ל (ועל פי פשוטו של מקרא):
עד כמה גדולה הכינות קיום המצות על ידי בני ישראל—שכמה
וכמה ענינים דלא שכיחי כלל וכלל—קרו ונעשו ובלבד שבני
ישראל יקיימו מצוה בשלימותה! ולא רק בעת קיום המצוה מסבב
הקדוש ברוך הוא שלא יהיו בלבולים ומניעות, אלא גם לפני בוא
הזמן לקיום המצוה בפועל, מסבב סיבות וכו'—בכדי שלאחרי זמן
רב—יהיה קיום מצוה בשלימותה. וכבנידון דידן, שהאדם והבהמה

שֶׁל מִדְיָן הָיָה כָּל אֶחָד וְאֶחָד מֵהֶם בְּמִסְפָּר מְדֻיָּק, בְּמֶשֶׁךְ זְמַן רַב לֹא
מֵת אַף אֶחָד אָדָם וְהַבְּהֵמָה וְכוּ ' ...

וּמִזֶּה הַהוֹרָאָה לְכָל אֶחָד וְאֶחָד: אֵין לְהִתְרַשֵּׁם מִכָּל בִּלְבּוּל וּמְנִיעָה
וְעִכּוּב, וְאִם לִפְעָמִים נִדְמָה כְּאִילוּ אֵין בִּיכוֹלֶת לְקַיֵּם מִצְוָה כוּ', אַל
יֵחוֹשׁ, אֶלָּא נָכוֹן יִהְיֶה לִבּוֹ בָּטוֹחַ שֶׁהַקָּדוֹשׁ בָּרוּךְ הוּא סִיבֵּב וְיְסַבֵּב
סִיבּוֹת וְעַד שֶׁיּוּכַל לְקַיֵּם הַמִּצְוָה בִּשְׁלֵימוּתָן.

The lesson is obvious:

A Jew's mitzvah is precious, so much so that extraordinary events that are completely uncommon occurred just so the Jews should be able to fulfill a mitzvah in the optimal manner! G-d doesn't just orchestrate events while the mitzvah is being performed; even before the mitzvah is actually fulfilled, G-d is pulling strings so that eventually, much later, the mitzvah could be fulfilled to its utmost. Look at our story—the people and cattle of Midian were exactly the number needed, and not a single one of them died for quite some time. . . .

The lesson to everyone should be clear: Do not be disheartened by any challenges to your divine service. Even if it seems that you are not able to fulfill a mitzvah, do not give up; rather be confident that G-d will orchestrate matters so that you will be able to fulfill the mitzvah in the best possible manner.

TEXT 10

Rabbi Sholom Dovber of Lubavitch, The Rebbe
Rashab, Sefer Hamaamarim 5657 p. 54

Rabbi Shalom Dovber Schneersohn
(Rashab)
1860–1920
Chasidic rebbe. Rabbi Shalom Dovber became the fifth leader of the Chabad movement upon the passing of his father, Rabbi Shmuel of Lubavitch. He established the Lubavitch network of *yeshivot* called Tomchei Temimim. He authored many volumes of chasidic discourses and is renowned for his lucid and thorough explanations of kabbalistic concepts.

ועל זה היה ירידת הנשמה למטה שירדה בגוף גשמי ובעולם גשמי אשר מוגבל מאד בהנהגת הטבע, ונראה ונדמה לו על פי חיצוניות הנהגת העולם שצריך להתנהג כך וכך דוקא, וכמו בעסק משא ומתן שנדמה בנפשו שצריך להשכים ולהעריב בו ולהיות כל היום בהעסק, ואם יקח שעה לעצמו להתפלל וללמוד תורה יפסיד בזה. וכמו כן נדמה לו שצריך לעשות תחבולות שונות בעניני העסק ואי אפשר לו להתנהג על פי האמת, שאם ילך על פי האמת לא ירויח או יפסיד כו' מפני שכללות הנהגת העולם מנגד לזה כו'.

אבל באמת לאמיתו אינו כן, דעצם הנהגת העולם מצד עצמו אינו מנגד לעסק תורה ועבודה וילך בדרכי האמת כו' ...כי אם תכלית הכוונה הוא שיעמוד נגד כל מונע ומעכב ויתפלל כדבעי ויעסוק בתורה בכל יום כפי הקביעות שיעשה לעצמו, ומדבר שקר ירחק וכן יזהר מתחבולות כי אם ילך בתום ובאמת ולא יהיה שום נדנוד איסור בעסקו במשא ומתן כו'.

The soul descended down to this earth and integrated within a corporeal body and a material world that is very limited, confined to its natural ways. The superficial, visible environment in this world conditions one to think that they must behave in a certain way.

Take business for example. The material environment conditions one to think that he must wake up early and go to sleep late, involved the entire day in his business. If he were to take an hour for himself to study and pray, surely he would lose money. He also is under the impression that he must game the system and use other tricks to make a buck; if he were to behave with absolute honesty, he would not be able to profit and instead incur losses. That's the way of the world. . . .

This cannot be further from the truth. By definition, the world does not oppose studying Torah, prayer, and integrity in business dealings. . . . The ultimate goal is for the person to stand up to all challenges and pray as he should, study Torah every day as per the set times he has set for himself, and to distance himself from any tricks, rather to deal honestly without any trace of dishonor in all of his business dealings.

TEXT 11

Rabbi Yehoshua Mondshein, Migdal Oz, pp. 177–178

תלמידו של רבנו הזקן – ר' מאיר רפאל'ס מווילנא – נסע פעם לרגל מסחרו בעגלתו עם הבעל עגלה המיוחד לו, ובאמצע הדרך הרגיש ר' מאיר כי אחת מציציותיו נפסלה. מיד ציוה לעגלון לעצור, כדי שלא להמשיך ללכת ד' אמות ללא טלית קטן עם ציצית כהלכתו. כך המתינו שעות ארוכות בציפייה, אולי יזדמן בדרך רוכל ובאמתחתו פתילי ציצית.

בין השמשות הבחינו ממרחק באדם הפוסע במהירות וחבילה על כתפו. ר' מאיר נתן קולו בצעקה גדולה, אך הלה נחפז לדרכו, ובדרך הילוכו, ניהל עם ר' מאיר את הדיאלוג הבא:

ואפילו אילו היו לי, כלום הייתי פורק את כל החבילה עבור כמה חוטים?! – כעס ההלך – רצוני להגיע העירה קודם חשיכה, ולא אתמהמה עבור זאת.

וגם אם אשלם במיטב כספי?

כמה, רובל?! לא כדאי לי!

ככל שתדרוש אשלם – הבטיח ר' מאיר!

אם כן – ניאות האיש – תן כל אשר בכוחך, את כל הכסף שבכיסך ובאמתחתך . . .

הזדרז ר' מאיר לרוקן את כיסיו, ונתן את כל אשר לו לידי הרוכל, ומיד הטיל הציצית בטליתו.

אחר תקופת זמן מה נסע ר' מאיר לרבנו הזקן. מיד עם כניסתו לחדרו של רבנו, קם הרבי ממקומו, הוציא מבין הספרים את כל המעות בשלמותן והחזירן לידי ר' מאיר . . . הלא זה לא היה אלא אליהו הנביא שנקרה בדרכו כדי להעמידו בנסיון.

Rabbi Meir Raphals, a disciple of the Alter Rebbe, once traveled in his special carriage on a business venture. On the way, Reb Meir realized that one of his tzitzit strings had become unkosher. He immediately instructed the wagon driver to stop, so that he not travel even four amot without a kosher pair of tzitzit. They waited for a good few hours, hoping that a traveling merchant would pass by and by chance have spare tzitzit.

As evening approached, they noticed a person on the horizon coming towards them with a bundle on his shoulders. Reb Meir called out loudly, but the man ignored him and seemed to continue on his way. As he was about to part ways, the travelling merchant engaged Reb Meir in the following conversation:

"And if I did have a few strings, do you think I would unload this heavy package for a few lousy threads? I want to get to town before sunset, and I won't be delayed for this!" he said angrily.

"Even if I pay you handsomely?" asked Reb Meir.

"How much? —a ruble? That's not worth it for me!"

Rabbi Meir promised, "Whatever you demand, I will pay!"

"If so," agreed the merchant, "Give me everything you have here; everything in your wallet and all your possessions."

Rabbi Meir quickly emptied his wallet, gave everything he had to the merchant, and immediately affixed the string to his tzitzit.

A while later, Rabbi Meir travelled to the Alter Rebbe. As soon as Rabbi Meir entered the room, the Alter Rebbe rose from his seat and took out all the money and returned it to Rabbi Meir. . . . Turns out, that "merchant" was Elijah the Prophet who had been sent to test Rabbi Meir.

3

DEVARIM

From Mourning to Morning

Between Misery and Bitterness, Despair and Progress

*Dedicated to **Mrs. Frumeth Polasky** in appreciation of her partnership in bringing the light of Torah to communities around the globe.*

PARSHAH OVERVIEW
Devarim

On the first of Shevat (thirty-seven days before his passing), Moses begins his repetition of the Torah to the assembled children of Israel, reviewing the events that occurred and the laws that were given in the course of their forty-year journey from Egypt to Sinai to the Promised Land, rebuking the people for their failings and iniquities, and enjoining them to keep the Torah and observe its commandments in the land that G-d is giving them as an eternal heritage, into which they shall cross after his death.

Moses recalls his appointment of judges and magistrates to ease his burden of meting out justice to the people and teaching them the word of G-d; the journey from Sinai through the great and fearsome desert; the sending of the spies and the people's subsequent spurning of the Promised Land, so that G-d decreed that the entire generation of the Exodus would die out in the desert. "Also against me," says Moses, "was G-d angry for your sake, saying: You, too, shall not go in there."

Moses also recounts some more recent events: the refusal of the nations of Moab and Ammon to allow the Israelites to pass through their countries; the wars against the Emorite kings Sichon and Og, and the settlement of their lands by the tribes of Reuben and Gad and part of the tribe of Manasseh; and Moses' message to his successor, Joshua, who will take the people into the Land and lead them in the battles for its conquest: "Fear them not, for the L-rd your G-d, He shall fight for you."

Day of Mourning

The History of the Ninth of Av

TEXT 1

Yirmiyahu (Jeremiah) 52:12

וּבַחֹדֶשׁ הַחֲמִישִׁי בֶּעָשׂוֹר לַחֹדֶשׁ הִיא שְׁנַת תְּשַׁע עֶשְׂרֵה שָׁנָה לַמֶּלֶךְ נְבוּכַדְרֶאצַּר מֶלֶךְ בָּבֶל בָּא נְבוּזַרְאֲדָן רַב טַבָּחִים עָמַד לִפְנֵי מֶלֶךְ בָּבֶל בִּירוּשָׁלָם:

And in the fifth month of Av, on the tenth of the month—that was the nineteenth year of the rule of King Nebuchadrezzar, King of Babylon—Nebuzaradan, the chief executioner, came and stood before the king of Babylon, in Jerusalem.

Different Dates

TEXT 2

Talmud Tractate Ta'anit 29a

וכתיב "ובחדש החמישי בעשור לחדש היא שנת תשע עשרה
[שנה] למלך נבוכדנצר מלך בבל בא נבוזראדן רב טבחים עמד לפני
מלך בבל בירושלם וגו'". ותניא: אי אפשר לומר בשבעה, שהרי כבר
נאמר בעשור; ואי אפשר לומר בעשור, שהרי כבר נאמר בשבעה.
הא כיצד? בשבעה נכנסו נכרים להיכל ואכלו וקלקלו בו שביעי
שמיני ותשיעי סמוך לחשכה הציתו בו את האור והיה דולק והולך
כל היום כולו, שנאמר "אוי לנו כי פנה היום כי ינטו צללי ערב".
והיינו דאמר רבי יוחנן אלמלי הייתי באותו הדור לא קבעתיו
אלא בעשירי מפני שרובו של היכל בו נשרף ורבנן אתחלתא
דפורענותא עדיפא.

Babylonian Talmud
A literary work of monumental proportions that draws upon the legal, spiritual, intellectual, ethical, and historical traditions of Judaism. The 37 tractates of the Babylonian Talmud contain the teachings of the Jewish sages from the period after the destruction of the Second Temple through the fifth century CE. It has served as the primary vehicle for the transmission of the Oral Law and the education of Jews over the centuries; it is the entry point for all subsequent legal, ethical, and theological Jewish scholarship.

The verse starts, "And in the fifth month, Av, on the seventh day of the month, being the nineteenth year of the reign Nebuchadnezzar King of Babylon, came Nebuzaradan, the Chief Executioner, servant of the King of Babylon, to Jerusalem, and he burnt the House of G-d."

Another verse states, "And in the fifth month of Av, on the tenth of the month—that was the nineteenth year of the rule of King Nebuchadrezzar, King of Babylon—Nebuzaradan, the chief executioner, came and stood before the king of Babylon, in Jerusalem."

The Sages taught: It is impossible to say the seventh of Av was the true date of destruction, since a verse says it was the tenth. However, it's also impossible to say the tenth was the true date, for a verse says it was the seventh. How do we resolve this contradiction? The enemy entered the Sanctuary on the seventh, and they ate and befouled it on the seventh, eighth, and ninth. Close to nightfall on the ninth, they set it on fire, and it burnt continuously all the entire day, as it is stated, "Woe to us, for the day has gone, for the shadows of the evening are stretched out."

This, then, is what Rabbi Yochanan said, "If I was alive in that generation, I would have established the day of mourning on the Tenth, as it was then that most of the Temple actually burned."

The Sages argue that the primary factor is when the calamity began [which was on the ninth].

Mourning Practices

TEXT 3

Shulchan Aruch Yoreh De'ah 394:1

שְׁלֹשָׁה יָמִים לִבְכִי, שִׁבְעָה לְהֶסְפֵּד, שְׁלֹשִׁים לְתִסְפֹּרֶת וּלְגִהוּץ.

Three days are set aside for weeping, seven for eulo-gizing, and thirty for cutting hair and pressing clothes.

TEXT 4A

Talmud Tractate Taanit 30a

תנו רבנן: כל מצות הנוהגות באבל נוהגות בט' באב אסור ברחיצה ובסיכה ובנעילת הסנדל ובתשמיש המטה ואסור לקרות בתורה בנביאים ובכתובים ולשנות במשנה בתלמוד ובמדרש ובהלכות ובאגדות.

The Sages taught: All the commandments we follow for mourning, we also follow on the Ninth of Av. It is forbidden to bathe, to anoint oneself, to wear leather shoes, or to engage in intimacy. It is also forbidden to read from the Torah, the Prophets, or the Writings (the Tanach), or to study the Mishnah, the Talmud, or the Midrash, whether Legal Midrash or Narrative Midrash.

Rabbi Yosef Caro
(Maran, *Beit Yosef*)
1488–1575
Halachic authority and author. Rabbi Caro was born in Spain but was forced to flee during the expulsion in 1492 and eventually settled in Safed, Israel. He authored many works including the *Beit Yosef*, *Kesef Mishneh*, and a mystical work, *Magid Meisharim*. Rabbi Caro's magnum opus, the Shulchan Aruch (Code of Jewish Law), has been universally accepted as the basis for modern Jewish law.

Differences

TEXT 4B

Ibid.

אבל קורא הוא במקום שאינו רגיל לקרות ושונה במקום שאינו רגיל
לשנות וקורא בקינות באיוב ובדברים הרעים שבירמיה ותינוקות
של בית רבן בטלין משום שנאמר "פקודי ה' ישרים משמחי לב".

*However, one may read parts of the Tanach one is
unaccustomed to reading and study parts of the Oral
Law one is not used to studying. One may read from
the book of Lamentations, and from Job, and from the
sad parts of Jeremiah. Even schoolchildren do not study
on Tishah Be'Av, since the verse says, "The commands
of G-d are right, and bring rejoicing to the heart."*

TEXT 5

Tosafot to Moed Katan 21a

"אסור לקרות בתורה". בתשובת רבינו יצחק זקני כתב כי רבינו יעקב
היה אוסר בימי אבלו באיוב ובקינות ובדברים הרעים שבירמיה
מדלא תני ליה בשמעתין כמו ט' באב שילהי תענית.

*It is forbidden for a mourner to read from the Torah.
In the responsa of Rabbi Yitzchak, my grandfather,
he wrote that Rabbi Yaakov, also known as Rabbeinu
Tam, forbade to a mourner even the books of Job,
Lamentations, and the sad parts of Jeremiah. He for-
bade them because they were not taught in this section
of the Talmud, dealing with mourners, as they were in
Tractate Ta'anit, about Tishah Be'Av.*

Tosafot

A collection of French
and German Talmudic
commentaries written
during the 12th and 13th
centuries. Among the
most famous authors of
Tosafot are Rabbi Yaakov
Tam, Rabbi Shimshon ben
Avraham of Sens, and Rabbi
Yitzchak ("the Ri"). Printed
in almost all editions of the
Talmud, these commentaries
are fundamental to basic
Talmudic study.

TEXT 6

Rabbi Asher Ben Yechiel, Piskei HaRosh Ta'anit §37

ומסתברא דחייב בתפילין אף על גב דהיא מצות לא תעשה כיון
דבאבל גופיה לא מיתסר אלא ביום ראשון ולא חמיר תשעה באב
משבעת ימי אבילות.

*It is logical to assume we are obligated to don the
tefilin on Tishah Be'Av, since the ban on wearing them
applies even to mourners only on the first day, and
Tishah Be'Av is certainly more lenient than the seven
days of mourning.*

Rabbi Asher ben Yechiel
(Rosh)
1250–1328

Rabbi, author, and Talmudist,
he is widely known by the
acronym "Rosh." Rabbi Asher
was a native of Germany,
where he was a prominent
disciple and successor of
Rabbi Meir (Maharam) of
Rothenburg. Due to the
persecution and massacres of
German Jewry under Emperor
Rudolph I, Rabbi Asher was
forced to flee, and in 1305,
he arrived in Toledo, Spain.
He is best known for his
halachic commentary on the
Talmud. Rabbi Asher was the
father of Rabbi Yaakov, the
author of the *Arbaah Turim*.

A Healthy System

TEXT 7

Talmud Tractate Yevamot 34b

אמר רב אשי שאני אבילות חדשה מאבילות ישנה (שאני בין
אבילות חדשה דתשעה באב דהוי אבילות ישנה ואבלות דברים
הלכך קילא. –רש"י)

Rav Ashi said: A new mourning differs from an old mourning. (Fresh mourning for a recent loss is unlike the old communal mourning of Tishah Be'Av, and thus Tishah Be'Av is more lenient. –Rashi)

The Correct Use of Sadness

Sadness with Positive Consequences

TEXT 8A

Mishlei (Proverbs) 14:23

בְּכָל עֶצֶב יִהְיֶה מוֹתָר וּדְבַר שְׂפָתַיִם אַךְ לְמַחְסוֹר:

In all suffering there is benefit, but the talk of the lips leads only to poverty.

TEXT 8B

Rabbi Shneur Zalman of Liadi, Tanya, ch. 26

ומה שכתוב בכל עצב יהיה מותר . . . מלשון זה משמע שהעצב
מצד עצמו אין בו מעלה רק שיגיע ויבא ממנו איזה יתרון והיינו
השמחה האמיתית בה' אלקיו הבאה אחר העצב האמיתי לעתים
מזומנים על עונותיו במר נפשו ולב נשבר.

*The verse states, "In all sadness there would be profit."…
The implication is that sadness has no inherent virtue,
rather that some profit is derived and experienced from*

Rabbi Shne'ur Zalman of Liadi (Alter Rebbe) 1745–1812

Chasidic rebbe, halachic authority, and founder of the Chabad movement. The Alter Rebbe was born in Liozna, Belarus, and was among the principal students of the Magid of Mezeritch. His numerous works include the *Tanya*, an early classic containing the fundamentals of Chabad Chasidism, and *Shulchan Aruch HaRav*, an expanded and reworked code of Jewish law.

it, *namely, the true joy in the Lord G-d which follows from genuine anguish over one's sins, at propitious moments with bitterness of soul and a broken heart.*

Lethargic Sadness vs. Energizing Bitterness

TEXT 9A

Tanya Chapter 31

אך באמת אין לב נשבר ומרירות הנפש על ריחוקה מאור פני ה'
והתלבשותה בסטרא אחרא נקראים בשם עצבות כלל בלשון
הקודש כי עצבות היא שלבו מטומטם כאבן ואין חיות בלבו אבל
מרירות ולב נשבר אדרבה הרי יש חיות בלבו להתפעל ולהתמרמר
רק שהיא חיות מבחינת גבורות קדושות והשמחה מבחינת חסדים
כי הלב כלול משתיהן.
והנה לעתים צריך לעורר בחינת גבורות הקדושות כדי להמתיק
הדינים שהם בחינת נפש הבהמית ויצר הרע כשישולט ח"ו על
האדם כי אין הדינים נמתקין אלא בשרשן.

"Depression" is not an appropriate term for the feeling one has when they are bitter and broken about the fact that they are distanced from G-d and steeped in materialism. "Depression" is when one's heart is hard like a rock, devoid of all life and spirit. "Bitterness" or "broken hearted" is quite the opposite—his heart is very much alive, animated and stirred to emotions

of bitterness. Such energy is different than the energy of joy and happiness which stems from chesed, but it is still energy—energy that stems from gevurah. The heart possesses both forms of energy.

At times, a person falls prey to his baser instincts and falls under their rule. At such times, a person must rouse his internal holy gevurot to ameliorate these forces, for such forces can only be sweetened at their source.

TEXT 9B

Ibid.

> ולכן אמרו רבותינו ז"ל "לעולם ירגיז אדם יצר הטוב" והיינו בכל עת שרואה בנפשו שצריך לכך. אך שעת הכושר שהיא שעה המיוחדת וראויה לכך לרוב בני אדם היא בשעה שהוא עצב בלאו הכי ממילי דעלמא או כך בלי שום סבה, אזי היא שעת הכושר להפך העצב להיות ממרי דחושבנא הנ"ל.

Therefore, the Rabbis, of blessed memory, said that, "A person should always excite the good nature," that is, whenever he perceives in his soul that he is in need of it. But the propitious time, which is the time specifically fitting for the majority of people, is when one is in any case troubled by mundane worries, or, simply, without apparent cause. Then is the appropriate time to transform the sadness by becoming one of those "masters of account" mentioned earlier.

Unlimited Joy, Defined Sadness

TEXT 10A

Mishnah Tractate Taanit 26b

משנכנס אב ממעטין בשמחה.

When the month of Av begins, we decrease in joy.

TEXT 10B

Shulchan Aruch, Orach Chayim 551:1–2

מראש חודש עד תענית ממעטים במשא ומתן ובבנין של שמחה
כגון בית חתנות לבנו או בנין של ציור וכיור ובנטיעת של שמחה
כגון אבורנקי של מלכים שנוטעים לצל להסתופף בצילו או מיני
הדס ומיני אהלים ואם היה כותלונוטה ליפול אף על פי שהוא של
שמחה מותר לבנות.
ואין נושאין נשים ואין עושין סעודה אירוסין.

*From Rosh Chodesh until the fast of Tishah Be'Av,
we reduce our business dealings and joyous building,
such as a father building a house for his bridegroom
son, or decorative building. We also do not perform
joyous planting, like planting a King's shady garden,
or myrtles, or tents. But if one's wall is about to fall,
even if it is in the category of joyous building, he may
build it.*

We do not get married during the month of Av, nor celebrate an engagement feast.

TEXT 10C

Talmud Tractate Taanit, 29a–b

משנכנס אב ממעטין בשמחה כו': אמר רב יהודה בריה דרב שמואל
בר שילת משמיה דרב כשם שמשנכנס אב ממעטין בשמחה כך
משנכנס אדר מרבין בשמחה.

"From when Av enters we decrease in joy." Rabbi Ye-huda the son of Rabbi Shmuel bar Sheilat said in the name of Rav: Just as when we enter Av we decrease in joy, so too when we enter Adar do we increase in joy.

TEXT 11

Rabbi Chaim Eliezer Shapiro of Munkacz, Shaar Yisaschar Adar Ch. 2

When we enter Adar, we increase in joy, but the Tal-mud does not tell us how we are supposed to increase it! It teaches us to increase joy almost as a tangential remark. But is there not a general principle that the positive is greater than the negative? Why would the

Talmud speak less about increasing joy than decreasing it?

Rather, to the contrary, this was an intentional omission on the part of the Sages. When it comes to decreasing joy, the Sages enumerated the specific means to do so, so that we would not mistakenly think we were obligated to be utterly dejected or depressed, G-d forbid.

In truth, utter dejection is no path for students of our master, the Baal Shem Tov of blessed memory, and those who follow them. (They are obligated to always be brokenhearted and grieving the exile and the destruction of the Temple, but never to be completely dejected to the point of despairing of the future redemption.) Joy is, in fact, a biblical commandment, "Since you did not serve me in joy…" Therefore, it is certainly forbidden to be completely dejected.

This is why the Sages established only the specific ways in which to decrease joy for the month of Av, in order to exclude all the other manners in which one is permitted to strengthen oneself with joy and trust in G-d, with a heart full of faith and looking forward to the redemption.

By contrast, when one enters Adar, there is no specific way in which to increase joy, because the positive is greater than the negative—there is no limit to this increase in joy, no area of life that is excluded from this mitzvah.

Happy Tishah Be'Av Customs

TEXT 12

Eichah (Lamentations) 5:21–22

> הֲשִׁיבֵנוּ ה' אֵלֶיךָ וְנָשׁוּבָה חַדֵּשׁ יָמֵינוּ כְּקֶדֶם:
> כִּי אִם מָאֹס מְאַסְתָּנוּ קָצַפְתָּ עָלֵינוּ עַד מְאֹד:

Return us to you, G-d, and we will be returned; renew our days as of old.

For You have truly rejected us and bitterly raged against us.

TEXT 13

Rabbi Moshe Isserles, Rama Orach Chaim 559:5

> ונוהגין לומר קצת נחמה אחר הקינות לפסוק בנחמה.

The custom is to speak some words of comfort after the words of mourning, so as to end on a comforting note.

Rabbi Moshe Isserlis (Rama)
1525–1572
Halachist. Rama served as rabbi in Krakow, Poland, and is considered the definitive authority on Jewish law among Ashkenazic Jewry. Rama authored glosses (known as the *Mapah*) on the Shulchan Aruch and *Darchei Moshe*, a commentary on the halachic compendium *Arbaah Turim*.

TEXT 14

The Lubavitcher Rebbe, Igrot Kodesh vol. 27 p. 142

Igrot Kodesh
A selection of Hebrew and Yiddish letters penned by the Rebbe. As of 2014, 30 volumes have been published in this series. The letters are published in chronological order, starting from 1925 and extending thus far to 1975. Only those letters that are of relevance to the public are published, and all personal information is excised. The letters cover a wide range of issues: communal activism, Chabad philosophy, Talmud, Jewish law, kabbalah, practical advice, and much more.

כשנופלים לאדם מחשבות והרהורי חרטה על הנהגה ומעשים בלתי רצוים ובתכיפות – צריך הוא לברר מאיזה "צד" באו: מיצרו הטוב, או ממנגדו. והבחינה העיקרית בזה – "תולדות" מחשבות אלו: באם המחשבות מולידות הוספת מרץ וחיות בקיום המצות, חיזוק בהנהגה יומית על פי שולחן ערוך (כולל – בנוגע אלי' – שמירת סדרי בית הספר וכו') – ראיה שמקורן טהור וטוב הוא. באם מולידות עצבות ורשלנות ועצלות או רגש של יאוש – הרי זו הוכחה שבאו מיצר הרע (אלא שנתלבש ונתחפש בלבוש של ירא שמים) כי כל אלו (עצבות וכו') מפריעים לאדם בעבודת השם.

When a person is constantly filled with thoughts and feelings of remorse over past misconduct, it is important to determine the source of these thoughts, whether they are emanating from the positive inclination [and as such should be acted upon], or from the evil inclination [and ought to be pushed aside].

The best way of determining this is by examining the consequences of these thoughts: if they lead to additional energy and vitality in the performance of mitzvos, conducting oneself to an even stronger degree according to Jewish law . . . then this is proof that these thoughts come from a good place.

If, by contrast, they lead to sadness and melancholy, neglect and laziness, or to feelings of hopelessness, then this is an indication that they come from the evil inclination (which has hid and donned garments of "piety"). For all the above hinder the individual in his divine service.

The Joy of Tishah Be'Av

Joy and Sadness: A Contradiction?

TEXT 15

Zohar vol. 2 p. 255a

בכיה תקיעא בלבאי מסטרא דא וחדוה תקיעא בלבאי מסטרא דא.

Weeping is lodged on one side of my heart and joy in the other.

Zohar

The seminal work of kabbalah, Jewish mysticism. The *Zohar* is a mystical commentary on the Torah, written in Aramaic and Hebrew. According to the Arizal, the *Zohar* contains the teachings of Rabbi Shimon bar Yocha'i, who lived in the Land of Israel during the second century. The *Zohar* has become one of the indispensable texts of traditional Judaism, alongside and nearly equal in stature to the Mishnah and Talmud.

The Fast's Permitted Celebration

TEXT 16A

Shulchan Melachim Pesicha L'Hilchos Tefilin, 15

On the second night of Yom Tov, many tzadikim, righteous men, are accustomed not to sit in the study hall, but rather in their homes, alone or in small numbers. It is also their custom that for the days at the beginning of Av, they finish tractates of the Talmud and eat feasts with meat and wine.

TEXT 16B

Ibid.

Both of these customs stem from the obligation and commandment to preempt the future redemption, when we will all live in Israel and the second day of Yom Tov, which is practiced only in exile, will no longer be observed. So, too, will the days of Av transform into days of joy in the future.

Not Mourning, but Energetic Resistance

TEXT 17

Rashi to Bereishit 37:35

**Rabbi Shlomo Yitzchaki
(Rashi)**
1040–1105
Most noted biblical and Talmudic commentator. Born in Troyes, France, Rashi studied in the famed *yeshivot* of Mainz and Worms. His commentaries on the Pentateuch and the Talmud, which focus on the straightforward meaning of the text, appear in virtually every edition of the Talmud and Bible.

"וַיְמָאֵן לְהִתְנַחֵם". אֵין אָדָם מְקַבֵּל תַּנְחוּמִין עַל הַחַי וְסָבוּר שֶׁמֵּת שֶׁעַל הַמֵּת נִגְזְרָה גְזֵרָה שֶׁיִּשְׁתַּכַּח מִן הַלֵּב, וְלֹא עַל הֶחָי.

"He refused to be comforted." One does not accept consolation for a living person presumed dead. Regarding the dead, G-d has decreed they will be forgotten from one's heart, but it has not been so decreed regarding the living.

TEXT 18

Rabbi Moshe Sofer, Derashot Chatam Sofer, v. 3, p. 84

The Sages tell us that Tishah Be'Av is called a holiday on which we do not say Tachnun *[supplicatory prayers]. How can it achieve the status a holiday, when, unlike every other holiday, we do not offer any holiday sacrifice to G-d?*

This can be understood by contemplating how for close to two thousand years during which we have been given all the blessings in the world, the Jewish people have yet to forget what happened on Tishah Be'Av, and have yet to dry our eyes from the tragedy. Every other nation and tongue that has lost has managed to forget their past calamities in light of their current blessings. Why are the Jewish people different?

We are different because we do not accept consolation for the living, whereas G-d decrees the dead to eventually be forgotten from one's heart. All the other nations have no hope to return to what they have lost, and therefore they forget. We, the Jewish people, still have hope, and await the day in the future when G-d will descend below, wreathed in flame, and his righteous ones will live again and see and be satisfied from his goodness.

We do not accept consolation for the living, and therefore, our mourning is actually for us the deepest

Rabbi Moshe Sofer
(Chatam Sofer)
1762–1839
A leading rabbinical authority of the 19th century. Born in Frankfurt am Main, *Chatam Sofer* ultimately accepted the rabbinate of Pressburg (now Bratislava), Slovakia. Serving as rabbi and head of the yeshiva that he established, Rabbi Sofer maintained a strong traditionalist perspective, opposing deviation from Jewish tradition. *Chatam Sofer* is the title of his collection of halachic responsa and his commentary to the Talmud.

comfort. It is called a great holiday, for it shows that we still know we will one day return to things as they were in the days of old, in our youth.

TEXT 19

Talmud Tractate Taanit 30b

"שמחו את ירושלם וגילו בה כל אוהביה שישו אתה משוש כל המתאבלים עליה". מכאן אמרו כל המתאבל על ירושלים זוכה ורואה בשמחתה ושאינו מתאבל על ירושלים אינו רואה בשמחתה.

The verse states, "Rejoice with Jerusalem and be glad with her, all who love her; rejoice for joy with her, all who mourn for her."

From this we learn: whoever mourns for Jerusalem merits to see her joy, and whoever does not mourn for Jerusalem does not see her joy.

4

VAETCHANAN—SHABBAT NACHAMU

Bringing out the Best

Looking at Challenge as Opportunity

*Dedicated to **Clive** and **Zoe Rock** in appreciation of their partnership in bringing the light of Torah to communities around the globe.*

PARSHAH OVERVIEW
Va'etchanan

Moses tells the people of Israel how he implored G-d to allow him to enter the Land of Israel, but G-d refused, instructing him instead to ascend a mountain and see the Promised Land.

Continuing his "review of the Torah," Moses describes the Exodus from Egypt and the Giving of the Torah, declaring them unprecedented events in human history. "Has there ever occurred this great thing, or has the likes of it ever been heard? Did ever a people hear the voice of G-d speaking out of the midst of the fire . . . and live? . . . You were shown, to know, that the L-rd is G-d . . . there is none else beside Him."

Moses predicts that in future generations the people will turn away from G-d, worship idols, and be exiled from their land and scattered amongst the nations; but from there they will seek G-d, and return to obey His commandments.

Our parshah also includes a repetition of the Ten Commandments, and the verses of the Shema, which declare the fundamentals of the Jewish faith: the unity of G-d ("Hear O Israel: the L-rd our G-d, the L-rd is one"); the mitzvot to love G-d, to study His Torah, and to bind "these words" as tefilin on our arms and heads, and inscribe them in the mezuzot affixed on the doorposts of our homes.

The Seven Haftarot of Consolation

TEXT 1A

Shulchan Aruch Orach Chaim 428:8

Rabbi Yosef Caro
(Maran, *Beit Yosef*)
1488–1575

Halachic authority and author. Rabbi Caro was born in Spain, but was forced to flee during the expulsion in 1492 and eventually settled in Safed, Israel. He authored many works including the *Beit Yosef*, *Kesef Mishneh*, and a mystical work, *Magid Meisharim*. Rabbi Caro's magnum opus, the Shulchan Aruch (Code of Jewish Law), has been universally accepted as the basis for modern Jewish law.

מי"ז בתמוז ואילך מפטירין ג' דפורענותא, ז' דנחמתא . . . ג'
דפורענותא; דברי ירמיהו, שמעו דבר ה', חזון ישעיהו. שבע דנחמתא,
נחמו, ותאמר ציון, עניה סוערה, אנכי, רני עקרה, קומי אורי,
שוש אשיש.

From the 17th of Tamuz and on, we read "three haftarot of punishment" and "seven haftarot of comfort"… the three haftarot of punishment are those beginning with, "Divrei yirmiyahu," "Shim'u devar hashem," and "Chazon yeshayahu." The seven Haftarot of Comfort are those beginning, "Nachamu," "Va'tomer tzion," "Aniyah soarah," "Anochi," "Rani akara," "Kumi ori and "Sos asis."

Gradual Consolation

TEXT 1B

Rabbi Simcha ben Shmuel of Vitry, Machzor Vitry h. 262

והאחרונות שכולן נחמה אומרים אותה מט' באב עד יום הכיפורים.
כדרך המנחמים לנחם מעט מעט. שהאומר לנחרב נחמה יותר מדאי
דומה כמי שאומר למחזיר על הפתחים למחר אתה מלך שאינו
מאמין. כמו שנאמר ולא שמעו אל משה מקוצר רוח ומעבודה וגו'.
לפיכך נחמו. ותאמר ציון. אף על פי שהיא נחרבת אל תאמר שהיא
נעזבת. ואחר כך עינייה. לפיכך הקדימוה לאנכי. אנכי אנכי הוא
מנחמכם. מאחר שניחמה הק' בחסדיו שוב אינו קורא לה נוחמה.
ועד כאן ניחמוה נביאים. מיכן ואילך הוא מנחמה. ואחר שקיבלה
תנחומים פוסק לה כמה טובות וגדולות: רני עקרה. קומי אורי.
שוש אשיש.

The final haftarah *portions, which all describe comfort-ing, are recited from the Ninth of Av until Yom Kippur. This accords with the way of comforters to comfort a little bit at a time. By contrast, overly comforting a grieving person can be likened to one who tells a beggar, "Tomorrow you will be a king," something the beggar will not believe. The matter is similar to the verse which states, "The Jewish people did not listen to Moses due to shortness of breath and hard labor," etc.*

Therefore, these haftarah *portions comfort gradually—first "Nachamu," and then "Va'tomer tzion," so as to* imply that although Jerusalem has been destroyed, just do not say it has been abandoned.

Afterword, we read the haftarah beginning, "Aniya." It precedes the haftarah of "Anochi," which implies that G-d Himself comforts. Thus concludes the comfort of the Prophets; henceforth G-d comforts.

Once the comfort has been accepted, the subsequent haftarot impart blessings of goodness and greatness, "Rani akara," "Kumi ori," and "Sos asis."

Double Vision

TEXT 2

Yeshayahu (Isaiah) 40:1

נַחֲמוּ נַחֲמוּ עַמִּי יֹאמַר אֱלֹקֵיכֶם:

"Console, console My people," says your G-d.

TEXT 3

Rabbi David Kimchi, Radak to Yeshayahu (Isaiah) 40:1

> "נחמו נחמו." כל אלה הנחמות עתידה לימות המשיח והכפל לחזק.

"Nachamu nachamu [Console, console]." All these comforts will take place in the era of Mashiach. The double language serves to strengthen the point.

Rabbi David Kimchi
(Radak)
1160–1235
Provencal medieval grammarian and biblical exegete. Rabbi Kimchi wrote a comprehensive exposition of Hebrew grammar called *Miklol*, and *Sefer Hashorashim*, a dictionary of the Bible. He is probably best known for his classic commentaries on the Bible.

Double Consolation for Double Pain

TEXT 4

Midrash Eicha Rabah 1:57

> חטאו בכפלים דכתיב חטא חטאה ירושלם, ולקו בכפלים, דכתיב כי לקחה מיד ה' כפלים בכל חטאתיה, ומתנחמים בכפלים, דכתיב נחמו נחמו עמי יאמר אלהיכם.

The Jewish people sinned doubly, as the verse states, "Jerusalem sinned grievously" [lit. Jerusalem sinned a sin]. They were doubly stricken, as the verse states, "For she has taken from the hand of G-d double for all her sins." And they are doubly comforted, as the verse states, "'Console, console My people,' says your G-d."

Eicha Rabah
A Midrashic text on the Book of Lamentations, produced by the sages of the Talmud in the Land of Israel. Its language closely resembles that of the Jerusalem Talmud. It was first printed in Pesaro, Italy, in 1519, together with four other Midrashic works on the other four *megilot*.

Isn't G-d Kind?

TEXT 5

Rabbi Shalom Dovber Schneersohn of Lubavitch, Sefer Hamaamarim 5672

Rabbi Shalom Dovber Schneersohn
(Rashab)
1860–1920

Chasidic rebbe. Rabbi Shalom Dovber became the fifth leader of the Chabad movement upon the passing of his father, Rabbi Shmuel of Lubavitch. He established the Lubavitch network of *yeshivot* called Tomchei Temimim. He authored many volumes of chasidic discourses and is renowned for his lucid and thorough explanations of kabbalistic concepts.

וצריך להבין מהו הכפילות דנחמו נחמו . . . ובמדרש רבה איתא לקתה בכפלים ונחמה בכפלים, ואינו מובן מהו ענין לקתה בכפלים, איך שייך שיהיה ח"ו העונש בכפליים על החטא, דבשלמא הנחמה בכפליים הוא מפני שמדה טובה מרובה כו', אבל מה שייך לקתה בכפלים כו', ומפני שלקתה בכפלים לכך ניחמה בכפלים צריך להבין מהו ענין הכפל כו'?

What is the meaning of the double language, "Console, console . . ."? Now, *Midrash Rabah* states that the Jewish people were doubly stricken and are doubly consoled. But what does that mean? How can there be double punishment for a sin, G-d forbid? It is understood how there can be double consolation, for, "A measure of goodness is greater than a measure [of punishment]," etc., but how is double punishment possible? And what does it mean that because the Jewish people were doubly stricken, they are doubly comforted? What is the meaning of this doubling?

Pass the Test, Bring out the Best

When G-d Tests

TEXT 6

Devarim (Deuteronomy) 13:4

לֹא תִשְׁמַע אֶל דִּבְרֵי הַנָּבִיא הַהוּא אוֹ אֶל חוֹלֵם הַחֲלוֹם הַהוּא כִּי מְנַסֶּה ה׳ אֱלֹקֵיכֶם אֶתְכֶם לָדַעַת הֲיִשְׁכֶם אֹהֲבִים אֶת ה׳ אֱלֹקֵיכֶם בְּכָל לְבַבְכֶם וּבְכָל נַפְשְׁכֶם:

You shall not heed the words of that prophet, or that dreamer of a dream; for the Lord, your G-d, is testing you, to know whether you really love the Lord, your G-d, with all your heart and with all your soul.

TEXT 7

Rabbi Shneur Zalman of Liadi, Likutei Torah, Reeh 19c

Rabbi Shneur Zalman of Liadi
(Alter Rebbe)
1745–1812
Chasidic rebbe, halachic authority, and founder of the Chabad movement. The Alter Rebbe was born in Liozna, Belarus, and was among the principal students of the Magid of Mezeritch. His numerous works include the *Tanya*, an early classic containing the fundamentals of Chabad Chasidism, and *Shulchan Aruch HaRav*, an expanded and reworked code of Jewish law.

דאין פירוש הפסוק לדעת הישכם אוהבים כו' שיהיה הקדוש ברוך הוא יודע כו' דאטו לנסיון הוא צריך כדי לדעת? —והלא הכל גלוי לפניו יתברך ויודע בראש מה שיהיה בסוף ומה שיבחור האדם.

The meaning of the verse is not that G-d is testing you so that He can know [whether you really love the Lord your G-d, etc.], for does G-d need to test us in order to know?! After all, isn't everything revealed before G-d, and He knows at the outset what the end will be and what man will choose?

Bringing out the Best

TEXT 8A

Ibid.

ותכלית ירידתה (של הנשמה) היא בשביל הנסיונות שבאין להאדם
שהם מהסתר פנים והסתלקות חיות השפע במניעת בריאת הגוף
או מניעת ממון כדי להסתיר על אור וחיות ה' וקדושתו יתברך
ולהיות מונע מבית ומבחוץ לאדם שבא להתקרב לה' ולעבודתו
יתברך כי דרך רשעים צלחה . . . וצריך האדם התגברות יתירה
לעמוד בנסיון שלא לחוש לשום מניעה ח"ו.

ובשביל כך באין לו הנסיונות כדי שיתגבר עליהם כדי שעל ידי כן
יבוא למעלת ומדרגת לדעת דהיינו שיהא אצלו בחינת דעת והשגה
והרגשה בו יתברך בבחינת ראיה.

*The purpose of the soul's descent into this world is to
be tried by tests which result from a concealment of
G-dliness, in the form of poor health or poverty, which
conceal G-d's light and distract a person from within
and without from coming close to G-d and His service,
for, "The way of the wicked has prospered" . . . a person needs extra fortitude to withstand the test and not
be intimidated by any obstacles, G-d forbid.*

*For this purpose, one is confronted by tests, so that
he may overcome them and thus reach the pinnacle
of divine connection, that one attain true knowledge,
perception, and feeling of G-d in a manner of seeing.*

When Father Hides

TEXT 8B

Ibid.

שהוא כמו שכתוב ואנכי הסתר אסתיר פני, כמו האב המסתיר את עצמו מבנו בכדי שהבן ירדוף אחריו ויתגלה חכמת הבן ודעתו החזקה שיבין שההסתר אינו אמיתי אלא רק בכדי שיבקשנו בחפש מחופש ואז ימצאנו וישמחו שניהם.

As the verse states, "And I will hide My face," like a father who hides from his son so that his son will chase after him. The father does this so that the son's wisdom will be revealed, and he will understand that the concealment is not real, rather merely to cause the son to search and then find him. And then, they will rejoice together.

The Fallen Wall

TEXT 9

Ibid.

והטעם שהנסיונות מביאין את האדם לידי דעת כי הנה הנסיונות הגם שירדו בהסתר פנים להיות מסתירים על חיות ה' וקדושתו יתברך הנה מוסתר בהם חיות אלקי . . .

והנה החיות אלקי שירד מטה מטה בהעלם והסתר פנים, יסודתו בהררי קדש ממקום גבוה מאד נעלה ממדרגות עליונות דקדושה כנודע ממשל נפילת החומה כו', אלא שנפל וירד מטה מטה בסתר המדרגות וכשעומד האדם בנסיון ומתגבר נגד כל מונע אזי קורע כל המסכים המסתירים ומעלימים אור וחיות ה' ונמצא שיוצא אור וחיות ה' מהעלם אל הגילוי ונמשך גילוי זה בנפשו להמשיך לה בחינת דעת והתגלות אלקותו יתברך.

The reason trials bring a person to divine connection is that although such trials are the result of a concealment of divine vitality and of His Holiness, in truth, within the trials is hidden divine vitality. . . .

Now, the divine vitality that has descended far below in a concealed fashion is rooted in an extremely lofty level of Supernal Holiness, as illustrated by the parable of the fallen wall, etc.; that vitality has merely fallen below in a concealed fashion. When a person withstands the tests and overcomes all obstacles, he tears away all masks that cover and conceal G-d's light and vitality, and the divine light and life leave their concealed state and are revealed. This revelation is revealed in the person's soul and draws down divine connection and a revelation of G-dliness.

Explaining the Doubles

Our Mission

Rabbi Menachem Mendel Schneerson
1902–1994

The towering Jewish leader of the 20th century, known as "the Lubavitcher Rebbe," or simply as "the Rebbe." Born in southern Ukraine, the Rebbe escaped Nazi-occupied Europe, arriving in the U.S. in June 1941. The Rebbe inspired and guided the revival of traditional Judaism after the European devastation, impacting virtually every Jewish community the world over. The Rebbe often emphasized that the performance of just one additional good deed could usher in the era of Mashiach. The Rebbe's scholarly talks and writings have been printed in more than 200 volumes.

TEXT 10A

The Rebbe, Rabbi Menachem Mendel Schneerson, Reshimot 13

אַךְ הִנֵּה בָּאָדָם הוּא שְׁלוּחוֹ שֶׁל הַקָּדוֹשׁ בָּרוּךְ הוּא בָּעוֹלָם.

Now, a person is G-d's agent in this world.

TEXT 10B

Babylonian Talmud
A literary work of monumental proportions that draws upon the legal, spiritual, intellectual, ethical, and historical traditions of Judaism. The 37 tractates of the Babylonian Talmud contain the teachings of the Jewish sages from the period after the destruction of the Second Temple through the fifth century CE. It has served as the primary vehicle for the transmission of the Oral Law and the education of Jews over the centuries; it is the entry point for all subsequent legal, ethical, and theological Jewish scholarship.

Talmud Tractate Kidushin, 42b

אֲבָל שַׁוֵּיהּ שָׁלִיחַ, אָמַר: לְתַקּוֹנֵי שְׁדַרְתִּיךְ וְלֹא לְעַוּוֹתִי.

If one appointed an agent he can say, "I sent you to act for my benefit and not to my detriment."

Two Meanings of Sin

TEXT 11A

Melachim I (I Kings) 1:21

וְהָיָה כִּשְׁכַב אֲדֹנִי הַמֶּלֶךְ עִם אֲבֹתָיו וְהָיִיתִי אֲנִי וּבְנִי שְׁלֹמֹה חַטָּאִים:

And [otherwise] when my lord the king shall sleep with his fathers, and I and my son Solomon shall be [considered] offenders (chata'im).

TEXT 11B

Rashi, ad loc.

"חטאים". חסרים ומנועין מן הגדולה כמו אל השערה ולא יחטיא.

"And I and my son Solomon shall be considered offenders (chata'im)." Instead they will always be lacking and restrained from any greatness.

Rabbi Shlomo Yitzchaki (Rashi)
1040–1105
Most noted biblical and Talmudic commentator. Born in Troyes, France, Rashi studied in the famed *yeshivot* of Mainz and Worms. His commentaries on the Pentateuch and the Talmud, which focus on the straightforward meaning of the text, appear in virtually every edition of the Talmud and Bible.

TEXT 12

Rabbi Shneur Zalman of Liadi, Likutei Torah, Matot 82a

וחטא הוא לשון חסרון ופגם שלשון חטא נופל אפילו על ביטול
מצות עשה ודקדוקי סופרים שעל כל פנים יש חסרון ופגם.

The word cheit *[lit. sin] connotes a deficiency and a blemish, for it applies even to one who neglects to do a positive command, and to one who neglects one of the Rabbinic details of a mitzvah. [Though one hasn't committed an actual sin] there is nevertheless a deficiency and a blemish.*

Punishment as a Cleanser

TEXT 13A

Talmud Tractate Makot 23a

כל חייבי כריתות שלקו נפטרו ידי כריתתם, שנאמר: ונקלה אחיך
לעיניך, כשלקה הרי הוא כאחיך דברי רבי חנניה בן גמליאל.

One who transgressed a sin whose punishment is karet *[punishment by premature death] but received lashes, is absolved from* karet, *as the verse states, "And your brother will be demeaned before you." Once he has been demeaned, he becomes like your brother. So are the words of Rabbi Chananya ben Gamliel.*

TEXT 13B

Maimonides, Mishneh Torah, Hilchot Sanhedrin 17:7

Rabbi Moshe ben Maimon
(Maimonides, Rambam)
1135–1204

Halachist, philosopher, author, and physician. Maimonides was born in Córdoba, Spain. After the conquest of Córdoba by the Almohads, he fled Spain and eventually settled in Cairo, Egypt. There, he became the leader of the Jewish community and served as court physician to the vizier of Egypt. He is most noted for authoring the *Mishneh Torah*, an encyclopedic arrangement of Jewish law, and for his philosophical work, *Guide for the Perplexed*. His rulings on Jewish law are integral to the formation of halachic consensus.

כל מי שחטא ולקה **חוזר לכשרותו** שנאמר "ונקלה אחיך לעיניך" כיון שלקה הרי הוא אחיך, אף כל מחוייבי כרת שלקו נפטרו מידי כריתתן.

Whenever a person sins and is lashed, he returns to his original state of acceptability, *as implied by the verse, "And your brother will be degraded before your eyes." Once he is lashed, he is "your brother."*

When Challenge Leads to More Challenge

TEXT 14

Talmud Tractate Eiruvin 41b

תנו רבנן: שלושה דברים מעבירין את האדם על דעתו ועל דעת קונו, אלו הן: עובדי כוכבים, ורוח רעה, ודקדוקי עניות. למאי נפקא מינה? למיבעי רחמי עלייהו.

The Sages taught: Three matters cause a person to act against his own will and the will of his Maker, and they are: idolaters, an evil spirit, and the depths of extreme poverty.

TEXT 15A

The Rebbe, Reshimot Ibid.

אבל בעונשים המונעים מקיום תורה ומצות [ולדוגמא] . . . דקדוקי
עניות שמעבירים על דעת קונו, שהאלקות לא בלבד שמייסר
על החטא, אלא שעוד מסייע בעשיית עבירה אחרת—הרי זה
לקתה בכפלים.

*With regards to punishments which prevent one from
observing Torah and mitzvot, [For example]…extreme
poverty, which causes a person to act against the will
of G-d. In this context, G-d is not only punishing the
perpetrator for the actual sin, He is assisting him to
perform yet another sin. This, then, is the meaning of
being "doubly stricken."*

The Greatest Test

TEXT 15B

Ibid.

כיון שחטאה בכפלים, היינו שלא בלבד שהיה העדר קיום השליחות,
אלא שמדעת עצמו עושה פעולות לקלקל גם מה שמתוקן, צריך
עצה ממה שלמעלה מסדר ההשתלשלות—נחמה בכפלים, שכר
בלי גבולי.
אלא שבכדי לבוא לזה צריך להיות ענין הנסיונות למעלה מטעם
ודעת והגבלות בני אדם, שכשעומד בזה ומבין שאין זה אלא

שאביו מתדמה כו' כדי לעורר כוחות הנעלמים של הבן—אזי זוכה
לנחמה בכפלים.
וזהו פירוש מארז"ל—שכיון שחטאה בכפלים, במילא לקתה
בכפלים, כדי שיבוא על ידי זה לנחמה בכפלים.

Since the nation sinned doubly, meaning it not only neglected to perform its mission, but of its own accord actively damaged what was already good, a remedy which transcends the regular spiritual order is required—a "double consolation," one which is unlimited.

But for this to occur, there must be trials that transcend logic and which defy human limits. When one withstands such tests, and understands that "his father is only pretending," as it were, to arouse the deepest abilities of the son—one merits a "double consolation."

This is the meaning of the Rabbis' teaching that because the Jewish people "sinned doubly," they were "doubly stricken"—so that they would ultimately be "doubly consoled."

5

EKEV

Where Is Your Passion?

Discovering What Really Makes You Tick

Dedicated to **Reb Zalman** and **Mimi Fellig** in appreciation of their partnership
in bringing the light of Torah to communities around the globe.

PARSHAH OVERVIEW
Ekev

In the parshah *of Ekev ("Because"), Moses continues his closing address to the children of Israel, promising them that if they will fulfill the commandments (mitzvot) of the Torah, they will prosper in the Land they are about to conquer and settle in keeping with G-d's promise to their forefathers.*

Moses also rebukes them for their failings in their first generation as a people, recalling their worship of the Golden Calf, the rebellion of Korach, the sin of the spies, their angering of G-d at Taveirah, Massah and Kivrot Hataavah ("The Graves of Lust"). "You have been rebellious against G-d," he says to them, "since the day I knew you." But he also speaks of G-d's forgiveness of their sins, and the Second Tablets which G-d inscribed and gave to them following their repentance.

Their forty years in the desert, says Moses to the people, during which G-d sustained them with daily manna from heaven, was to teach them "that man does not live on bread alone, but by the utterance of G-d's mouth does man live."

Moses describes the land they are about to enter as "flowing with milk and honey," blessed with the "seven kinds" (wheat, barley, grapevines, figs, pomegranates, olive oil and dates), and as the place that is the focus of G-d's providence of His world. He commands them to destroy the idols of the land's former masters, and to beware lest they become haughty and begin to believe that "my power and the might of my hand have gotten me this wealth."

A key passage in our parshah is the second chapter of the Shema, which repeats the fundamental mitzvot enumerated in the Shema's first chapter, and describes the rewards of fulfilling G-d's commandments and the adverse results (famine and exile) of their neglect. It is also the source of the precept of prayer, and includes a reference to the resurrection of the dead in the messianic age.

Moshe's Worry

Recounting the Golden Calf

TEXT 1

Devarim (Deuteronomy) 8:7–17

זְכֹר אַל תִּשְׁכַּח אֵת אֲשֶׁר הִקְצַפְתָּ אֶת ה' אֱלֹקֶיךָ בַּמִּדְבָּר לְמִן הַיּוֹם אֲשֶׁר יָצָאתָ מֵאֶרֶץ מִצְרַיִם עַד בֹּאֲכֶם עַד הַמָּקוֹם הַזֶּה מַמְרִים הֱיִיתֶם עִם ה':

וּבְחֹרֵב הִקְצַפְתֶּם אֶת ה' וַיִּתְאַנַּף ה' בָּכֶם לְהַשְׁמִיד אֶתְכֶם:

בַּעֲלֹתִי הָהָרָה לָקַחַת לוּחֹת הָאֲבָנִים לוּחֹת הַבְּרִית אֲשֶׁר כָּרַת ה' עִמָּכֶם וָאֵשֵׁב בָּהָר אַרְבָּעִים יוֹם וְאַרְבָּעִים לַיְלָה לֶחֶם לֹא אָכַלְתִּי וּמַיִם לֹא שָׁתִיתִי:

וַיִּתֵּן ה' אֵלַי אֶת שְׁנֵי לוּחֹת הָאֲבָנִים כְּתֻבִים בְּאֶצְבַּע אֱלֹקִים וַעֲלֵיהֶם כְּכָל הַדְּבָרִים אֲשֶׁר דִּבֶּר ה' עִמָּכֶם בָּהָר מִתּוֹךְ הָאֵשׁ בְּיוֹם הַקָּהָל:

וַיְהִי מִקֵּץ אַרְבָּעִים יוֹם וְאַרְבָּעִים לָיְלָה נָתַן ה' אֵלַי אֶת שְׁנֵי לֻחֹת הָאֲבָנִים לֻחֹת הַבְּרִית:

וַיֹּאמֶר ה' אֵלַי קוּם רֵד מַהֵר מִזֶּה כִּי שִׁחֵת עַמְּךָ אֲשֶׁר הוֹצֵאתָ מִמִּצְרָיִם סָרוּ מַהֵר מִן הַדֶּרֶךְ אֲשֶׁר צִוִּיתִם עָשׂוּ לָהֶם מַסֵּכָה:

וַיֹּאמֶר ה' אֵלַי לֵאמֹר רָאִיתִי אֶת הָעָם הַזֶּה וְהִנֵּה עַם קְשֵׁה עֹרֶף הוּא: הֶרֶף מִמֶּנִּי וְאַשְׁמִידֵם וְאֶמְחֶה אֶת שְׁמָם מִתַּחַת הַשָּׁמָיִם וְאֶעֱשֶׂה אוֹתְךָ לְגוֹי עָצוּם וָרָב מִמֶּנּוּ:

וָאֵפֶן וָאֵרֵד מִן הָהָר וְהָהָר בֹּעֵר בָּאֵשׁ וּשְׁנֵי לֻחֹת הַבְּרִית עַל שְׁתֵּי יָדָי:

וָאֵרֶא וְהִנֵּה חֲטָאתֶם לַה' אֱלֹקֵיכֶם עֲשִׂיתֶם לָכֶם עֵגֶל מַסֵּכָה סַרְתֶּם מַהֵר מִן הַדֶּרֶךְ אֲשֶׁר צִוָּה ה' אֶתְכֶם:

וָאֶתְפֹּשׂ בִּשְׁנֵי הַלֻּחֹת וָאַשְׁלִכֵם מֵעַל שְׁתֵּי יָדָי וָאֲשַׁבְּרֵם לְעֵינֵיכֶם:

Remember, do not forget how you angered the Lord, your G-d, in the desert; from the day that you went out of the land of Egypt, until you came to this place, you have been rebelling against G-d.

At Horeb, you angered G-d, and G-d was incensed with you to destroy you.

When I ascended the mountain to receive the stone tablets, the tablets of the covenant which G-d made with you, I remained on the mountain forty days and forty nights; I neither ate bread nor drank water.

And G-d gave me two stone tablets, inscribed by the finger of G-d, and on them was [inscribed] according to all the words that the Lord spoke with you on the mountain from the midst of the fire on the day of the assembly.

And it came to pass at the end of forty days and forty nights, that G-d gave me two stone tablets, the tablets of the covenant.

And G-d said to me, "Arise, descend quickly from here, for your people whom you have brought out of Egypt have become corrupt; they have quickly deviated from the way which I commanded them; they have made for themselves a molten image."

And G-d spoke to me [further], saying, "I have seen this people, and, behold, it is a stiff-necked people.

Leave Me alone, and I will destroy them and obliterate their name from beneath the heavens, and I will make you into a nation mightier and more numerous than they."

So I turned and came down from the mountain, and the mountain was burning with fire, and the two tablets of the covenant were on my two hands.

And I saw, and behold, you had sinned against the Lord, your G-d; you had made yourselves a molten calf; you had deviated quickly from the way which the Lord had commanded you.

So I grasped the two tablets, cast them out of my two hands, and shattered them before your eyes.

TEXT 1B

Ibid., v. 18–19

וָאֶתְנַפַּל לִפְנֵי ה' כָּרִאשׁנָה אַרְבָּעִים יוֹם וְאַרְבָּעִים לַיְלָה לֶחֶם לֹא
אָכַלְתִּי וּמַיִם לֹא שָׁתִיתִי עַל כָּל חַטַּאתְכֶם אֲשֶׁר חֲטָאתֶם לַעֲשׂוֹת
הָרַע בְּעֵינֵי ה' לְהַכְעִיסוֹ:
כִּי יָגֹרְתִּי מִפְּנֵי הָאַף וְהַחֵמָה אֲשֶׁר קָצַף ה' עֲלֵיכֶם לְהַשְׁמִיד אֶתְכֶם
וַיִּשְׁמַע ה' אֵלַי גַּם בַּפַּעַם הַהִוא:

And I fell down before G-d as before, forty days and forty nights; I neither ate bread nor drank water, because of all your sins you had committed, by doing evil in the eyes of G-d to anger Him.

For I was frightened of the wrath and the fury that G-d was angry with you to destroy you, and the Lord hearkened to me also at that time.

TEXT 2A

Shemot (Exodus) 32:7–19

וַיְדַבֵּר ה' אֶל מֹשֶׁה לֶךְ רֵד כִּי שִׁחֵת עַמְּךָ אֲשֶׁר הֶעֱלֵיתָ מֵאֶרֶץ מִצְרָיִם:
סָרוּ מַהֵר מִן הַדֶּרֶךְ אֲשֶׁר צִוִּיתִם עָשׂוּ לָהֶם עֵגֶל מַסֵּכָה וַיִּשְׁתַּחֲווּ לוֹ
וַיִּזְבְּחוּ לוֹ וַיֹּאמְרוּ אֵלֶּה אֱלֹהֶיךָ יִשְׂרָאֵל אֲשֶׁר הֶעֱלוּךָ מֵאֶרֶץ מִצְרָיִם: . . .
וַיְחַל מֹשֶׁה אֶת פְּנֵי ה' אֱלֹהָיו וַיֹּאמֶר לָמָה ה' יֶחֱרֶה אַפְּךָ בְּעַמֶּךָ אֲשֶׁר
הוֹצֵאתָ מֵאֶרֶץ מִצְרַיִם בְּכֹחַ גָּדוֹל וּבְיָד חֲזָקָה: . . .
וַיִּנָּחֶם ה' עַל הָרָעָה אֲשֶׁר דִּבֶּר לַעֲשׂוֹת לְעַמּוֹ:
וַיִּפֶן וַיֵּרֶד מֹשֶׁה מִן הָהָר וּשְׁנֵי לֻחֹת הָעֵדֻת בְּיָדוֹ לֻחֹת כְּתֻבִים מִשְּׁנֵי
עֶבְרֵיהֶם מִזֶּה וּמִזֶּה הֵם כְּתֻבִים:
וְהַלֻּחֹת מַעֲשֵׂה אֱלֹהִים הֵמָּה וְהַמִּכְתָּב מִכְתַּב אֱלֹהִים הוּא חָרוּת
עַל הַלֻּחֹת:
וַיִּשְׁמַע יְהוֹשֻׁעַ אֶת קוֹל הָעָם בְּרֵעֹה וַיֹּאמֶר אֶל מֹשֶׁה קוֹל
מִלְחָמָה בַּמַּחֲנֶה:
וַיֹּאמֶר אֵין קוֹל עֲנוֹת גְּבוּרָה וְאֵין קוֹל עֲנוֹת חֲלוּשָׁה קוֹל עֲנוֹת
אָנֹכִי שֹׁמֵעַ:
וַיְהִי כַּאֲשֶׁר קָרַב אֶל הַמַּחֲנֶה וַיַּרְא אֶת הָעֵגֶל וּמְחֹלֹת וַיִּחַר אַף מֹשֶׁה
וַיַּשְׁלֵךְ מִיָּדָיו אֶת הַלֻּחֹת וַיְשַׁבֵּר אֹתָם תַּחַת הָהָר:

And G-d said to Moses, "Go, descend, for your people that you have brought up from the land of Egypt have acted corruptly.

They have quickly turned away from the path that I have commanded them; they have made themselves a molten calf! And they have prostrated themselves before it, slaughtered sacrifices to it, and said: 'These are your gods, O Israel, who have brought you up from the land of Egypt.'"...

Moses pleaded before the Lord, his G-d, and said: "Why, O Lord, should Your anger be kindled against Your people whom You have brought up from the land of Egypt with great power and with a strong hand?

G-d [then] reconsidered the evil He had said He would do to His people.

Now Moses turned and went down from the mountain [bearing] the two tablets of the testimony in his hand, tablets inscribed from both their sides; on one side and on the other side they were inscribed.

Now the tablets were G-d's work, and the inscription was G-d's inscription, engraved on the tablets.

When Joshua heard the voice of the people in their shouting, he said to Moses, "There is a voice of battle in the camp!"

But [Moses] said: "[It is] neither a voice shouting victory, nor a voice shouting defeat; a voice of blasphemy I hear."

Now it came to pass when he drew closer to the camp and saw the calf and the dances, that Moses' anger was kindled, and he flung the tablets from his hands, shattering them at the foot of the mountain.

TEXT 3

Jerusalem Talmud Tractate Shekalim 6:1

רבי שמואל בר נחמני אמר: הלוחות ארכן ששה טפחים, ורחבן ששה טפחים, והיה משה תופס בטפחיים, והקדוש ברוך הוא בטפחיים, וטפחיים ריווח באמצע. וכיון שעשו ישראל אותו מעשה, ביקש הקדוש ברוך הוא לחטפן, גברו ידיו של משה וחטפן. הוא שהקדוש ברוך הוא משבחו "ולכל היד החזקה", יהא שלמא לידה דגברא על ימינא.

Rabbi Shmuel bar Nachmani said: The tablets were six handbreadths long and six handbreadths wide; Moses was holding onto two handbreadths, and G-d was holding on to two handbreadths, leaving two handbreadths in the middle.

When the Jews sinned [with the golden calf], G-d tried to grab them, but Moses hands' overcame and he grabbed them. On this account G-d praised Moses saying, ". . . And all the strong hand"—peace unto the hand that overpowered My right hand.

TEXT 4

Nachmanides, Ramban al Hatorah, Devarim (Deuteronomy) 9:19

כי יגרתי מפני האף - יאמר כי מפני האף והחמה אשר קצף השם
מתחלה עליכם להשמיד אתכם יגורתי גם עתה, כי עדיין יש עליכם
להשמיד אתכם מן הקצף הגדול ההוא אף על פי שכבר נחם השם
על הרעה אשר דבר לעשות לעמו. על כן חזרתי והתנפלתי עליכם
ארבעים יום וארבעים לילה, עד ששמע אלי גם בפעם ההיא כאשר
שמע בפעם הראשונה קודם שירדתי . . . כי עד שיבער את העגל
לא השגיח רק להשיב חמתו מהשחית את העם כרגע.

*"For I was frightened by the wrath." Because of the
wrath and the fury that G-d was angry with you to
destroy you, I was afraid now as well. G-d still had
reason to destroy you due to that original great wrath,
although G-d already decided not to do to his people
the evil He had spoken.*

*Therefore I once again fell before Him on your behalf
for forty days and forty nights, until He listened to me
once again, as He had listened to me before I descended
the mountain the first time . . . For before the calf was
destroyed, G-d had only agreed not to destroy the nation in an instant.*

Still Questions

TEXT 5

Midrash Tehilim 7

אמר רבי שמואל בר נחמני בשעה שעלה משה למרום וסרחו
ישראל, נזדווגו לו חמשה מלאכי חבלה, ואלו הן. אף וקצף וחימה
והשמד ומשחית. אף זה מלאך הממונה על האף, וחימה זה מלאך
החימה, וקצף זה מלאך הקצף, ומשחית זה מלאך המשחית,
והשמד זה מלאך המשמיד.

והיה משה מתיירא מהם, ונתלה בזכות אבות העולם. אמר לפניו
רבונו של עולם זכור לאברהם ליצחק ולישראל עבדיך . . . מיד
נתמלא הקדוש ברוך הוא רחמים, שנאמר וינחם ה' על הרעה. מיד
נסתלקו מישראל שלשה מלאכי חבלה קצף ומשחית ומשמיד.
מנין שנשתלחו בישראל אף וחימה, שנאמר כי יגורתי מפני האף
והחמה. אמר לפניו רבונו של עולם לית אנא יכול למיקם בתרוייהון,
קום את בחד ואנא בחד, חדא הוא דכתיב קומה ה' באפך, ומנין
שעמד משה בחימה, שנאמר ויאמר להשמידם לולי משה בחירו
וגו' להשיב חמתו.

Rabbi Shmuel bar Nachmani said: When Moses ascended the mountain and the Jews sinned, five angels of destruction appeared to him: Af, Ketzef, Cheimah, Hashmed and Mashchit. Mashchit is a destructive angel, and Hashmed is an even more destructive angel.

Moses was afraid of them, and he invoked the merit of the Forefathers. He said, "Master of the Universe, remember Abraham, Isaac and Israel your servants . . ."

and immediately, G-d was filled with compassion, as the verse continues, "G-d [then] reconsidered the evil [He had said He would do to His people]. Immediately, three of the destructive angels departed from Israel, Ketzef, Mashchit, and Mashmid.

How do we know that Af and Cheima were dispatched to Israel? The verse states, "For I was frightened of the wrath and the fury [mipnei ha'af vehacheima]." Moses said, "Master of the Universe, I cannot stand up to both of them. You rise up to one and I will rise up to the other. This is the meaning of the verse, "Arise, O G-d, in your wrath." And regarding Moses standing up to Cheima, the verse states, "He intended to destroy them [and would have] were it not that Moses, His chosen one, [stood before Him in the breech] to return His wrath from destroying."

Three for Three

What's in a Soul

TEXT 5

Midrash Bereishit Rabah, 14:9

חמשה שמות נקראו לה: נפש, רוח, נשמה, יחידה, חיה.

The soul is called by five names: Nefesh, Ruach, Neshama, Yechida, and Chaya.

TEXT 6

Rabbi Yehuda Loew, The Maharal of Prague, Tiferet Yisrael ch. 1

כי באדם שלושה דברים: הגוף והנפש והשכל, ובכל שלושתן משמש האדם בהם לצורך חיותו.

Man is comprised of three parts: the body, the soul, and the intellect. Man uses each of these three to live.

Three Parts of the Sin

TEXT 7

Shemot (Exodus) 32:7–8

וַיְדַבֵּר ה' אֶל מֹשֶׁה לֶךְ רֵד כִּי שִׁחֵת עַמְּךָ אֲשֶׁר הֶעֱלֵיתָ מֵאֶרֶץ מִצְרָיִם:
סָרוּ מַהֵר מִן הַדֶּרֶךְ אֲשֶׁר צִוִּיתִם עָשׂוּ לָהֶם עֵגֶל מַסֵּכָה וַיִּשְׁתַּחֲווּ לוֹ
וַיִּזְבְּחוּ לוֹ וַיֹּאמְרוּ אֵלֶּה אֱלֹהֶיךָ יִשְׂרָאֵל אֲשֶׁר הֶעֱלוּךָ מֵאֶרֶץ מִצְרָיִם:

And G-d said to Moses, "Go, descend, for your people that you have brought up from the land of Egypt have acted corruptly.

They have quickly turned away from the path that I have commanded them; they have made themselves a molten calf! And they have prostrated themselves before it, slaughtered sacrifices to it, and said: 'These are your gods, O Israel, who have brought you up from the land of Egypt.'"

The Gateway Sin

TEXT 8

Midrash Shemot Rabah 42

ויקומו לצחק אין מצחק אלא עבודה זרה ואין מצחק אלא גילוי
עריות ואין מצחק אלא שפיכות דמים.

"They got up to sport." Sport refers to idolatry, forbidden relations, and murder.

Eroding Three Foundations

TEXT 9A

Mishnah Tractate Avot 1:2

שמעון הצדיק היה משירי כנסת הגדולה הוא היה אומר על שלשה
דברים העולם עומד על התורה ועל העבודה ועל גמילות חסדים:

Shimon the Righteous was among the last surviving members of the Great Assembly. He would say: The world stands on three things: Torah, the service of G-d, and deeds of kindness.

TEXT 9B

Rabbi Yehuda Loewe, the Maharal of Prague, Derech Chaim 1:2

ומן הדברים אשר בארנו יש לך להבין מה שאמרו ז"ל כי כל העבירות שבתורה יעבור ואל יהרג חוץ עבודה זרה [גילוי עריות] ושפיכות דמים . . . טעם דבר זה, כי אלו ג' עבירות הם הפך אלו ג' דברים שהעולם עומד עליהם, כי אין ספק כי עבודה זרה הפך העבודה שהיא אל השם יתברך, ושפיכות דמים היא הפך גמילות חסדים, כי זה מטיב לאחר ועושה לו דבר שאין צריך לעשות, ושפיכות דמים מאבדו לגמרי.

וגלוי עריות הוא הפך התורה כי כבר בארנו למעלה כי מעלת התורה שהיא השכל נבדל מן חמרי לגמרי, ואין דבר שעל ידו האדם נבדל מן החמרי רק על ידי התורה השכלית ואין צריך לזה ראיה, והפך זה גילוי עריות שהולך אחר זנות שהיא גם כן ובזה הולך אחר החמרי עד שהוא נחשב לגמרי כמו בהמה וחמור . . . כי הזנות מעשה בהמה חמרית . . . ולפיכך הזנות של גלוי עריות הוא הפך מדריגת התורה שהיא תורה שכלית והזנות מעשה חמרי.

The Sages state, "With regard to all other transgressions in the Torah, [if a person is told: Transgress this prohibition and you will not be killed,] he may transgress that prohibition and not be killed, with the exception of idol worship, forbidden sexual relations, and bloodshed." This is because these three sins are the antitheses of the "three things upon which the world stands." Undoubtedly, idol worship is the opposite of worshipping G-d, and bloodshed is the opposite of kind deeds. A kind person goes out of his way to do something for another person, whereas bloodshed destroys another person entirely.

And forbidden relations are the opposite of Torah . . . for Torah is utterly abstract from physical matter. Only the intellect of Torah elevates a person above corporeality; this doesn't require proof. By contrast, when a person deviates with forbidden relations, he follows corporeality completely, to the point that he is like an animal and a donkey . . . Forbidden relations is an animalistic, material matter . . . Deviating with forbidden relations is the opposite of the level of Torah, which is an intellectual Torah, while forbidden relations are an entirely physical matter.

Antidote to the Big Three

TEXT 10

Ibid.

ותדע כי אלו שלשה דברים שהם התורה והעבודה וגמילת חסדים,
כמו שהיו אלו ג' דברים ג' עמודי עולם, נתנו לג' אבות שהם אברהם
יצחק ויעקב שהם גם כן יסודות ואבות העולם, ולכך ראוי שיהיה
להם אלו ג' דברים שהם יסודות ועמודים לעולם. וזה כי תמצא
גמילת חסדים שהיה מדת אברהם. כמו שמבואר בכתוב שהיה זריז
בכל גמילת חסדים, דהיינו קבלת אורחים . . .
יצחק זכה במדת העבודה שהרי הקריב עצמו על גבי מזבח . . .
יעקב היה לו מדת התורה כמו שאמר יעקב איש תם יושב אוהלים.

Now, these three things upon which the world stands, which are Torah, Divine Service, and kind deeds, were given to the three Patriarchs, Abraham, Isaac, and Jacob, who are likewise pillars and forefathers of the world. Therefore, it is befitting for them to possess the three pillars of the world.

As we find, Abraham embodied kind deeds; he was energetically involved with welcoming guests. . . . Isaac merited the realms of Divine Service; he was offered up on the altar. . . . Jacob merited the realm of Torah, as the verse states, "Jacob was an innocent man, dwelling in tents."

Back to the Angels

TEXT 11A

Rabbi Shmuel Bornsztain of Sochatchov, Shem Mishmuel Ekev 5675

ונראה שמצד קלקול ג' אלה נתהוו ג' מיני מלאכי חבלה קצף
משחית ומכלה ואלה מקבילים לנוכח אלה:
בשביל קלקול השכל נתהוה קצף שכל קצפון הוא היפוך כח השכלי
וישוב הדעת, והקצף מסלק השכל ...
בשביל קלקול הנפש נתהוה משחית, כי השחתה היא קלקול
הצורה שהיא הנפש של החומר, על כן השחתה מתיחסת לנפש ...
ובשביל קלקול הגוף נתהוה מכלה, כי כליון מתיחס לגוף וחומר
וגשם כענין שכתוב וכלתו ואת עציו ואת אבניו ... וכאלה
רבים במקרא.
ואם כן מובן שמחמת שלשה חטאים אלו השתחואה, זביחה
ואמירה, שמהם נעשה הקלקול בגוף ונפש ושכל, נתהוו מהם ג'
מלאכי חבלה אלה קצף משחית ומכלה.

I would like to suggest that the three angels of destruction,
Ketzev, Mashchit, and Mechaleh, correspond to, and
were the product of, sinning with man's three elements:

For defiling the intellect, Ketzef (anger) was created,
which represents the opposite of logic and clear think-
ing. Anger drives away intellect. . . .

For defiling the soul, Mashchit (destruction) was
created, which represents the defilement of the form
which is the soul of the material. As such, hashchata
[corruption or destruction] relates to the soul. . . .

And for defiling the body, Mechale (eradication) was created, which represents the body and matter and corporeality, as the verse states, "and eradicate him, and his wood, and his stones."...

If so, it is understood that for the three sins of prostration, slaughtering, and proclamation, which defiled the body, soul, and intellect, the three destructive angels Ketzef, Mashchit, and Mechale were created.

TEXT 11B

Ibid.

אך קמה כנגדם זכות ג' אבות שהם היפוך עבודה זרה גילוי עריות ושפיכת דמים כמבואר במהר"ל ותקנו חטא אדם הראשון בעבודה זרה גילוי עריות ושפיכת דמים, על כן ברחו או אתכליאו מפני זכותם קצף משחית ומכלה, ועל זה כתיב וינחם ה' על הרעה אשר דיבר לעשות לעמו.

The merit of the three Forefathers, which represents the antitheses of idolatry, incest, and murder, stood up against these three angels; as the Maharal has explained, the Forefathers rectified Adam's sin of idolatry, incest, and murder. Therefore the three angels Ketzef, Mashchit and Mechale either fled or were destroyed in the presence of our Forefathers' merits. Regarding this, the verse states, "G-d [then] reconsidered the evil He had said He would do to His people."

The Power of Joy

What Moses Saw

TEXT 12

Rabbi Ovadia Seforno, Shemot 32:19

וירא את העגל ומחולות ויחר אף משה. כשראה שהיו שמחים
בקלקול שעשו, כענין כי רעתכי אז תעלזי ובזה התקצף ונואש שיוכל
לתקון המעוות באופן שיחזרו לתמותם ויהיו ראוים לאותן הלוחות.

"[When he drew closer to the camp and] saw the calf
and the dances, Moses' anger was kindled." When he
saw that they were rejoicing over their sin, as in the
verse, "for [with] your evil then you rejoice," he grew
angry and lost hope that he might be able to rectify the
sin in a way that they would return to their innocence
and be deserving of the tablets.

When Dancing Led to Despair

TEXT 13

Rabbi Shmuel Bornsztain, Shem Mishmuel ibid.

דעד כה לא ידע רק מהשתתחואה וזביחה ואמירה שסיפר לו השם
יתברך, שהם בגוף ונפש ושכל, הוה ידע שפיר שזכות ג' האבות
תעמוד להם, ועל כן התאמץ בכל עוז לחטוף את הלוחות, באשר
חשב שסוף כל סוף יתרצה הקדוש ברוך הוא להם בזכות ג' האבות
ואז ימסרם להם, אך כאשר ראה את העגל ומחולות, והיינו השמחה
שהיתה להם, אז נתיאש מלתקן שיהיו ראויים ללוחות אלו.

Thus far, Moses was only aware of their sin of prostration, slaughtering, and proclamation, of which G-d had told him. These pertain to the body, soul, and intellect, and Moses knew that the merit of the three Forefathers would come to their aid. Therefore, he tried with all his might to grab the tablets, with the assumption that ultimately, G-d would forgive them in the merit of the Forefathers and then be willing to give the tablets to the Jewish people. But when "he saw the calf and the dances," i.e., their joy, he despaired of being able to rectify the situation so that they'd be befitting to receive these tablets.

Transcendental Joy

TEXT 14

Rabbi Shalom DovBer Schneersohn of Lubavitch,
Sefer Hamaamarim 5697, p. 174

ואנו רואים דכל מי שישמח באיזה שמחה הרי הוא מגלה כל לבבו
בדבור ובתנועת האיברים וכו' . . . עד שלא יוכל להעלים כל דבר
בעצמו מצד השמחה ומגלה כל מצפוני לבבו כו'.

We observe that whenever someone rejoices over something, he reveals his entire heart with his words and by the movement of his limbs, etc. . . . to the point that he cannot contain anything, due to his great joy, but rather reveals all that is hidden in his heart, etc.

TEXT 15

Siddur Tefilot Mikol Hashana, Shaar Hasukot, p. 299

אבל תחילת קבלת התענוג בלבבו יהיה בהסתר והצנע רק יתעדן
בעצמותו ואחר כך ירצה לגלות עונג שלו ויזמין רבים שישמחו
גם הם בשמחתו ושיאכלו וישתו עמו. והנה נראה בחוש שמבקש
ומפציר גם השונאים שלו שיאכלו וישתו עמו וישמחו בשמחתו
מפני שבשעת שמחת לבו נולדה מחדש אהבה להשונא אף שהיה
בלבבו טינא אליו מחמת הרעות שעשה לו, הנה עתה בשמחתו
שהוא למעלה מהשכל בטלה הטעם והשכל שגרמו הטינא וכלא
חשיבי וממשיך לו אהבה אמיתי ורוצה וחפץ באמת שיאכל וישתה
וישמח עמו.

At first, one's pleasure is felt hidden in his heart, he rejoices to himself. Afterwards, he wishes to express his pleasure, and will invite many others to rejoice together with him, to eat and drink. We see clearly that a person will even encourage those he hates to eat and drink and rejoice with him, for when he is happy, he feels a new sense of love to this person, despite previously harbored ill-feeling toward him due to the wrongs that he has committed. But now, as he experiences joy which transcends intellect, the rationale that led to the ill-feelings are nullified and considered as naught. Rather, he extends true love and truly wishes for this person to eat, drink, and rejoice with him.

The Remaining Two Angels

TEXT 16A

Shem Mishmuel, Ibid.

מחמת חטא ההוללות והשמחה, שהן קלקול בחינות חי' ויחידה
שבנפש, נתהוו עוד שני מיני מלאכי חבלה והם אף וחימה, כמו
שהשמחה וההוללות היו כוללין כל חלקי האדם עד שיכול לסבול
כנ"ל, כן להיפוך כח האף והחימה הוא נמי כולל כל חלקי האדם,
ועל כן נתהוה מכח השמחה וההוללות עוד שני מלאכי חבלה אלו
אף וחימה והם ב' הקשים באשר הם לעומת חלקי הנפש היותר
גבוהים ומהם נתירא משה ביותר.

*From the sin of their rejoicing, which defile the levels of
Chaya and Yechidah in the soul, two more destructive
angels were created: Af and Cheima. Just as joy envel-
ops a person entirely, to the point that he can tolerate
[something he usually hates], so, too, the power of Af
and Cheima envelop the entire person. Therefore from
their joy was created these two more angels, Af and
Cheima, which are the two harshest ones in that they
correspond to the highest levels of the soul. It was these
angels that Moses so greatly feared.*

6

REEH

Emulating Your Creator

Work Isn't Just about the Money

*Dedicated to **Asher** and **Michelle Milstein** in appreciation of their partnership
in bringing the light of Torah to communities around the globe.*

PARSHAH OVERVIEW
Re'eh

"See," says Moses to the people of Israel, "I place before you today a blessing and a curse"—the blessing that will come when they fulfill G-d's commandments, and the curse if they abandon them. These should be proclaimed on Mount Gerizim and Mount Ebal when the people cross over into the Holy Land.

A Temple should be established in "the place that G-d will choose to make dwell His name there," where the people should bring their sacrifices to Him; it is forbidden to make offerings to G-d in any other place. It is permitted to slaughter animals elsewhere, not as a sacrifice but to eat their meat; the blood (which in the Temple is poured upon the altar), however, may not be eaten.

A false prophet, or one who entices others to worship idols, should be put to death; an idolatrous city must be destroyed. The identifying signs for kosher animals and fish, and the list of non-kosher birds (first given in Leviticus 11), are repeated.

A tenth of all produce is to be eaten in Jerusalem, or else exchanged for money with which food is purchased and eaten there. In certain years this tithe is given to the poor instead. Firstborn cattle and sheep are to be offered in the Temple, and their meat eaten by the kohanim (priests).

The mitzvah of charity obligates a Jew to aid a needy fellow with a gift or loan. On the Sabbatical year (occurring every seventh year), all loans are to be forgiven. All indentured servants are to be set free after six years of service.

Our parshah concludes with the laws of the three pilgrimage festivals—Passover, Shavuot and Sukkot—when all should go to "see and be seen" before G-d in the Holy Temple.

Why Work
The Requirement to Do

TEXT 1A

Devarim (Deuteronomy) 15:18

לֹא יִקְשֶׁה בְעֵינֶךָ בְּשַׁלֵּחֲךָ אֹתוֹ חָפְשִׁי מֵעִמָּךְ כִּי מִשְׁנֶה שְׂכַר שָׂכִיר
עֲבָדְךָ שֵׁשׁ שָׁנִים וּבֵרַכְךָ ה' אֱלֹהֶיךָ בְּכֹל אֲשֶׁר תַּעֲשֶׂה:

You shall not be troubled when you send him free from you, for twice as much as a hired servant, he has served you six years, and the Lord, your G-d, will bless you in all that you shall do.

TEXT 1B

Sifrei ad loc.

Sifrei
An early rabbinic Midrash on the biblical books of Numbers and Deuteronomy. *Sifrei* focuses mostly on matters of law, as opposed to narratives and moral principles. According to Maimonides, this halachic Midrash was authored by Rav, a 3rd-century Babylonian Talmudic sage.

"וברכך ה' אלקיך." יכול אפילו עומד ובטל? תלמוד לומר בכל
אשר תעשה.

"The Lord your G-d will bless you." Perhaps this applies even if one stands idly? The verse therefore teaches "in all that you do."

Parental Responsibilities

TEXT 2

Talmud Tractate Kiddushin, 29a

דתנו רבנן: האב חייב בבנו למולו ולפדותו וללמדו תורה ולהשיאו
אשה וללמדו אומנות. ויש אומרים אף להשיטו במים. רבי יהודה
אומר כל שאינו מלמד את בנו אומנות מלמדו ליסטות. ליסטות
סלקא דעתך? אלא כאילו מלמדו ליסטות.

Babylonian Talmud
A literary work of monumental proportions that draws upon the legal, spiritual, intellectual, ethical, and historical traditions of Judaism. The 37 tractates of the Babylonian Talmud contain the teachings of the Jewish sages from the period after the destruction of the Second Temple through the fifth century CE. It has served as the primary vehicle for the transmission of the Oral Law and the education of Jews over the centuries; it is the entry point for all subsequent legal, ethical, and theological Jewish scholarship.

The Sages taught in a beraita: A father is obligated to circumcise his son, to redeem him if he is a firstborn, to teach him Torah, to marry him off to a woman, and to teach him a trade. And some say: [A father is also obligated to teach his son] to swim.

Rabbi Yehuda says: Any father who does not teach his son a trade teaches him banditry [listut].

Can it enter your mind that he actually teaches him banditry?!

Rather, [the beraita means] that it is as though he teaches him banditry.

Side Jobs for Scholars

TEXT 3A

Pirkei Avot 2:2

Ethics of the Fathers
(*Pirkei Avot*)
A six-chapter work on Jewish ethics that is studied widely by Jewish communities, especially during the summer. The first five chapters are from the Mishnah, tractate Avot. Avot differs from the rest of the Mishnah in that it does not focus on legal subjects; it is a collection of the sages' wisdom on topics related to character development, ethics, healthy living, piety, and the study of Torah.

רַבָּן גַּמְלִיאֵל בְּנוֹ שֶׁל רַבִּי יְהוּדָה הַנָּשִׂיא אוֹמֵר, יָפֶה תַלְמוּד תּוֹרָה עִם דֶּרֶךְ אֶרֶץ, שֶׁיְּגִיעַת שְׁנֵיהֶם מְשַׁכַּחַת עָוֹן. וְכָל תּוֹרָה שֶׁאֵין עִמָּהּ מְלָאכָה, סוֹפָהּ בְּטֵלָה וְגוֹרֶרֶת עָוֹן.

Rabban Gamliel the son of Rabbi Judah HaNasi would say: Beautiful is the study of Torah with the way of the world, for the toil of them both causes sin to be forgotten. Ultimately, all Torah study that is not accompanied with work is destined to cease and to cause sin.

TEXT 3B

Rabeinu Yonah, Avot ad loc.

Rabbi Yonah of Gerona
d. 1263
Spanish rabbi and Talmudist. Rabbeinu Yonah from Gerona, Catalonia, was a cousin of Nachmanides. He is renowned for his outspoken critique of Maimonides's works, and for later recanting his opposition and vowing to travel to Maimonides's grave in Israel to beg his forgiveness. He left France, but was detained in Toledo, Spain, where he stayed and became one of the greatest Talmudists of his time. He is best known for his moralistic works on repentance and asceticism

וכל התורה שאין עמה מלאכה סופה בטלה. כענין שאמרו במכילתין "אם אין קמח אין תורה". העניין כמשמעו כשיתבטל ממלאכה מביאתו אל העוני וגוררת כמה עונות ורעתה רבה כי מפניה יאהב מתנות ולא יחיה. ויחניף בני אדם אף אם הם רשעים כדי שיתנו לו. גם כי יתם הכסף מהמתנות יהיה גנב או קוביוסטוס ויביא גזלות העני לביתו לבל ימות ברעב. ובהגיע אדם אל המדות האלה אין מעצר לרוחו ולא ינוח ולא ישקוט עד יעבור על כל המצות האמורות בתורה כי עבירה גוררת עבירה.

ועל זה אמרו רז"ל במסכת חולין "כל הנהנה מיגיעו עליו הכתוב
אומר 'יגיע כפיך כי תאכל אשריך וטוב לך'. אשריך בעולם הזה וטוב
לך לעולם (הבא)." על כן צריך לחכם שידע מלאכה כענין שנאמר
"טובה חכמה עם נחלה".

"All Torah study that is not accompanied with work is destined to cease." As the Sages have said, "If there is no flour, there is no Torah." The matter is to be taken literally—joblessness leads to poverty, which leads to many sins, and to great evil, for one will come to rely on gifts...He will resort to flattery, even of the wicked, so that they will provide for him. Furthermore, when the gifted funds are finished, he will become a thief or a gambler who takes from other poor people in order to avoid starvation. When a person reaches such a state, there is no stopping his spirit; he will not rest or be tamed until he transgresses all the mitzvot of the Torah, for one sin leads to another.

Regarding this have the Sages said, "Anyone who subsists on his own toil, upon him can be applied the verse, 'If you eat the toil of your hands, you are praiseworthy, and it is good for you.'" You are praiseworthy in this World, and it will be good for you in the World to Come. Therefore a wise person must know a trade, as the verse states, "Wisdom is good with a heritage."

The Career Conundrum

TEXT 4A

Rabbi Shalom DovBer of Lubavitch, Kuntres Uma'ayon, ch.17

Rabbi Shalom Dovber Schneersohn
(Rashab)
1860–1920

Chasidic rebbe. Rabbi Shalom Dovber became the fifth leader of the Chabad movement upon the passing of his father, Rabbi Shmuel of Lubavitch. He established the Lubavitch network of *yeshivot* called Tomchei Temimim. He authored many volumes of chasidic discourses and is renowned for his lucid and thorough explanations of kabbalistic concepts

וְהָעִנְיָן הוּא דְהִנֵּה כְּתִיב וּבֵרַכְךָ ה' אֱלֹקֶיךָ בְּכֹל אֲשֶׁר תַּעֲשֶׂה, וְצָרִיךְ לְהָבִין לָמָּה צְרִיכִים הָעֲשִׂיָּה וְהָעֵסֶק כְּלָל מֵאַחַר שֶׁהַבְּרָכָה מֵאֵת ה' תָּבֹא אִם כֵּן גַּם בְּלִי עֵסֶק וְהִשְׁתַּדְּלוּת כְּלָל תָּבֹא בִּרְכַּת ה', וּמִמַּה שֶׁאוֹמֵר בְּכֹל אֲשֶׁר תַּעֲשֶׂה מַשְׁמַע שֶׁצָּרִיךְ לִהְיוֹת עֲשִׂיָּה וְעֵסֶק, וּבְיוֹתֵר אֵינוֹ מוּבָן לְפִי מַה שֶׁאָמְרוּ רַבּוֹתֵינוּ זִכְרוֹנָם לִבְרָכָה כָּל מְזוֹנוֹתָיו שֶׁל אָדָם קְצוּבִים לוֹ מֵרֹאשׁ הַשָּׁנָה עַד יוֹם הַכִּפּוּרִים, וְאִם כֵּן מַהוּ הַצּוֹרֶךְ לַעֲסוֹק בְּאֵיזֶה מַשָּׂא וּמַתָּן אוֹ אוּמָנוּת שֶׁעַל יְדֵי זֶה יִתְפַּרְנֵס, הֲלֹא וַדַּאי מַה שֶׁנִּקְצְבָה לוֹ פַּרְנָסָה בְּחֶסֶד עֶלְיוֹן יִמְשַׁךְ לוֹ וְלָמָּה צָרִיךְ עֵסֶק וְהִשְׁתַּדְּלוּת בָּזֶה.

The verse states, "The Lord your G-d will bless you in all that you do." Now, why is such action and toil necessary to begin with, inasmuch as blessings come from G-d? If that is the case, let G-d's blessing come without toil and effort at all. Yet the fact that the verse states "in all that you do" indicates that there must be deed and toil.

The matter is even more difficult to understand when we consider the saying of our Sages that, "A person's livelihood is determined between Rosh Hashanah and Yom Kippur." If so, what need is there to work in any type of business or craft to earn money? Certainly the livelihood established by G-d's kindness will come to be, so why should one have to work for it?

Making a "Vessel"

TEXT 5A

Ibid ch.25

שֶׁצְּרִיכָה לִהְיוֹת עֲשִׂיָּה וְהַיְינוּ הֲכָנַת כְּלִי שֶׁל פַּרְנָסָה, דְּזֶהוּ א'
הַהֶבְדֵּלִים בֵּין זְמַן הַגָּלוּת בַּעֲבוֹדַת הַבֵּירוּרִים וּבֵין הַזְּמַן דְּלֶעָתִיד
בְּבִיאַת הַמָּשִׁיחַ, דְּלֶעָתִיד הִנֵּה שֶׁפַע חֶסֶד הָעֶלְיוֹן יָבֹא מֵאִתּוֹ יִתְבָּרֵךְ
בְּלֹא שׁוּם הִתְעַסְּקוּת וַהֲכָנַת כְּלִי עֵסֶק בִּשְׁבִיל פַּרְנָסָה, מַה שֶּׁאֵין כֵּן
בִּזְמַן הַגָּלוּת צְרִיכִים הִתְעַסְּקוּת בַּהֲכָנַת כְּלִי לְפַרְנָסָה, וְטַעַם הַדָּבָר
שֶׁצְּרִיכָה לִהְיוֹת עֲשִׂיָּה דַּוְקָא הוּא מֵאַחַר שֶׁהַהַשְׁפָּעָה צְרִיכָה לִהְיוֹת
נִמְשֶׁכֶת עַל יְדֵי לְבוּשֵׁי הָעֲשִׂיָּה עַל כֵּן גַּם הָאָדָם אַתֶּם שֶׁהוּא בְּדֻגְמָא
שֶׁלְּמַעְלָה צָרִיךְ גַּם כֵּן לַעֲשׂוֹת לְבוּשׁ וְעֵסֶק פַּרְנָסָה שֶׁבָּזֶה תִּתְלַבֵּשׁ
הַבְּרָכָה שֶׁלְּמַעְלָה בִּלְבוּשֵׁי הַטֶּבַע.

There must be action on our part, which creates a vehicle for livelihood. This is one of the differences between work done during exile vs. the era of Moshiach. When Moshiach comes, Supernal Kindness will flow with no effort or toil for livelihood on our part. But currently, we must work and create a channel for our livelihood. The reason there must be action on our part is because the Supernal Kindness must flow through the channels of nature. Therefore, man must also act and toil to earn a livelihood so that G-d's blessing be integrated into the rules of nature.

TEXT 5B

Ibid.

וּבֶאֱמֶת הִנֵּה כָּל אֵלֶּה לְבוּשֵׁי הַטֶּבַע אֵינָם אֶלָּא לְבוּשׁ לְבָד אֲבָל הַבְּרָכָה נִמְשֶׁכֶת מִלְמַעְלָה עַל יְדֵי הַלְּבוּשׁ וְלֹא מִצַּד עַצְמוּת הַלְּבוּשׁ חַס וְשָׁלוֹם, וּכְמוֹ שֶׁגִּדוּל הַתְּבוּאוֹת נִמְשָׁךְ עַל יְדֵי הַשֶּׁמֶשׁ וְהַיָּרֵחַ וּכְמוֹ שֶׁכָּתוּב וּמִמֶּגֶד תְּבוּאוֹת שָׁמֶשׁ וּמִמֶּגֶד גֶּרֶשׁ יְרָחִים וְעִם זֶה אֵינָן אֶלָּא שְׁלוּחֵי הַהַשְׁפָּעָה וְאֵין בְּיָדָם לְהָרַע וּלְהֵטִיב כִּי אִם אֶת אֲשֶׁר יֹאמַר הַקָּדוֹשׁ בָּרוּךְ הוּא, וּכְמוֹ שֶׁנִּתְבָּאֵר לְעֵיל, כַּךְ הָעֵסֶק וְהַלְּבוּשׁ הוּא רַק כִּשָׁלִיחַ לְבָד וְהַהַשְׁפָּעָה הִיא בְּיַד הַקָּדוֹשׁ בָּרוּךְ הוּא.

The reality is that all these natural means are nothing more than a ploy; the blessing flows from Above through a certain vehicle, but does not flow from the vehicle itself, G-d forbid. Growth of crops is affected by the sun and moon, yet it is readily understood that the sun and moon are nothing more than the messengers of G-d who have no authority to harm nor help, but rather can do nothing more than what they are commanded by G-d... A person's business dealings and natural means of earning a livelihood are merely an agent; the flow of sustenance from above is determined by of G-d, blessed be He.

Don't Lose Focus

TEXT 5C

Ibid.

וּלְפִי זֶה מוּבָן שֶׁאֵין צְרִיכִים לְהַאֲרִיךְ בְּהַלְבוּשׁ יוֹתֵר מִדַאי כִּי זֶה לְלֹא צוֹרֶךְ מֵאַחַר שֶׁלֹא הַלְבוּשׁ הוּא הָעִיקָר כִּי אִם הַשְׁפָּעָתוֹ יִתְבָּרֵךְ שֶׁמַשְׁפִּיעַ עַל יְדֵי הַלְבוּשׁ, וְאִם כֵּן הָעִיקָר הוּא שֶׁיִּתְפַּלֵל לְמִי שֶׁהָעוֹשֶׁר וְהַנְכָסִים שֶׁלוֹ וִיַשֵׁר דַרְכוֹ בְּדֶרֶךְ הַתּוֹרָה וְהַמִצְוֹת שֶׁיִּהְיֶה רָאוּי לְבִרְכַּת ה' וְהַשְׁפָּעַת חֶסֶד, וְהַיְינוּ שֶׁיוּמְשַׁךְ לוֹ קִצְבַת הַחֶסֶד בְּרֹאשׁ הַשָׁנָה וְיוֹם הַכִּפּוּרִים עַל יְדֵי קַבָּלַת עוֹל מַלְכוּתוֹ יִתְבָּרֵךְ וְעַל יְדֵי תְּשׁוּבָתוֹ הָאֲמִיתִּית

It is thus understood that we ought not to spend too much time on the agent, for that would be a futile exercise. Because one's goal is G-d's blessing and the business is merely the agent, it follows that his focus should be on praying to He who truly possesses wealth and property, and on following the ways of the Torah and the mitzvot, so as to be worthy of G-d's blessing and kindness that were fixed for him through his acceptance of G-d and through his true repentance on Rosh Hashanah and Yom Kippur.

Human Dignity

Born to Work

TEXT 6

Iyov (Job) 5:7

כִּי אָדָם לְעָמָל יוּלָד וּבְנֵי רֶשֶׁף יַגְבִּיהוּ עוּף:

Man was born to work but flying creatures fly upward.

Earning Your Keep

TEXT 7A

Talmud Bava Metzia 39a

אמר רב כהנא אדם רוצה בקב שלו מתשעה קבים של חבירו.

Rav Kahana said: A person prefers a kav [an ancient measurement] of his own produce to nine kav of another's produce.

TEXT 7B

Rashi ad loc.

חביבה עליו על ידי שעמל בהן וקב שישאר לו מהם הוא רוצה, מתשעה קבין של אחרים שיקח בדמיהן אם ימכרם.

One's produce is dear to him because it is the product of his toil. He would prefer one kav that remains from his own work even if he could potentially sell it and with the proceeds purchase nine kav of someone else's produce.

Rabbi Shlomo Yitzchaki (Rashi)
1040–1105
Most noted biblical and Talmudic commentator. Born in Troyes, France, Rashi studied in the famed *yeshivot* of Mainz and Worms. His commentaries on the Pentateuch and the Talmud, which focus on the straightforward meaning of the text, appear in virtually every edition of the Talmud and Bible.

TEXT 7C

Nachmanides, Milchamot Hashem, ad loc.

מפני שאדם נהנה כשאוכל מיגיעו ומקיים ביה יגיע כפיך כי תאכל אשריך וטוב לך.

A person derives pleasure from eating of his own efforts and thereby fulfilling the verse, "If you eat the toil of your hands, you are praiseworthy, and it is good for you."

Rabbi Moshe ben Nachman (Nachmanides, Ramban)
1194–1270
Scholar, philosopher, author, and physician. Nachmanides was born in Spain and served as leader of Iberian Jewry. In 1263, he was summoned by King James of Aragon to a public disputation with Pablo Cristiani, a Jewish apostate. Though Nachmanides was the clear victor of the debate, he had to flee Spain because of the resulting persecution. He moved to Israel and helped reestablish communal life in Jerusalem. He authored a classic commentary on the Pentateuch and a commentary on the Talmud

Giving Discreetly

TEXT 8

Maimonides, Mishneh Torah, Laws of Presents to the Poor 10:7–14

שמנה מעלות יש בצדקה זו למעלה מזו, מעלה גדולה שאין למעלה ממנה זה המחזיק ביד ישראל שמך ונותן לו מתנה או הלואה או עושה עמו שותפות או ממציא לו מלאכה כדי לחזק את ידו עד שלא יצטרך לבריות לשאול, ועל זה נאמר והחזקת בו גר ותושב וחי עמך כלומר החזק בו עד שלא יפול ויצטרך.

פחות מזה הנותן צדקה לעניים ולא ידע למי נתן ולא ידע העני ממי לקח, שהרי זו מצוה לשמה, כגון לשכת חשאים שהיתה במקדש, שהיו הצדיקים נותנין בה בחשאי והעניים בני טובים מתפרנסין ממנה בחשאי, וקרוב לזה הנותן לתוך קופה של צדקה, ולא יתן אדם לתוך קופה של צדקה אלא אם כן יודע שהממונה נאמן וחכם ויודע להנהיג כשורה כר' חנניה בן תרדיון.

פחות מזה שידע הנותן למי יתן ולא ידע העני ממי לקח, כגון גדולי החכמים שהיו הולכין בסתר ומשליכין המעות בפתחי העניים, וכזה ראוי לעשות ומעלה טובה היא אם אין הממונין בצדקה נוהגין כשורה.

פחות מזה שידע העני ממי נטל ולא ידע הנותן, כגון גדולי החכמים שהיו צוררים המעות בסדיניהן ומפשילין לאחוריהן ובאין העניים ונוטלין כדי שלא יהיה להן בושה.

פחות מזה שיתן לו בידו קודם שישאל.

פחות מזה שיתן לו אחר שישאל.

פחות מזה שיתן לו פחות מן הראוי בסבר פנים יפות.

פחות מזה שיתן לו בעצב.

There are eight levels of charity, each greater than the next.

The greatest level, above which there is no greater, is to support a fellow Jew by endowing him with a gift or loan, or entering into a partnership with him, or finding employment for him, in order to strengthen his hand so that he will not need to be dependent upon others . . .

A lesser level of charity than this is to give to the poor without knowing to whom one gives, and without the recipient knowing from who he received. For this is performing a mitzvah solely for the sake of Heaven. This is like the "anonymous fund" that was in the Holy Temple [in Jerusalem]. There the righteous gave in secret, and the good poor profited in secret. Giving to a charity fund is similar to this mode of charity, though one should not contribute to a charity fund unless one knows that the person appointed over the fund is trustworthy and wise and a proper administrator, like Rabbi Chananyah ben Teradyon.

A lesser level of charity than this is when one knows to whom one gives, but the recipient does not know his benefactor. The greatest Sages used to walk about in secret and put coins in the doors of the poor. It is worthy and truly good to do this, if those who are responsible for distributing charity are not trustworthy.

A lesser level of charity than this is when one does not know to whom one gives, but the poor person does know his benefactor. The greatest Sages used to tie coins into their robes and throw them behind their backs, and the poor would come up and pick the coins out of their robes, so that they would not be ashamed.

A lesser level than this is when one gives to the poor person directly into his hand, but gives before being asked.

A lesser level than this is when one gives to the poor person after being asked.

A lesser level than this is when one gives inadequately, but gives gladly and with a smile.

A lesser level than this is when one gives unwillingly.

TEXT 9A

Talmud Tractate Ketubot 67b

תנו רבנן: אין לו ואינו רוצה להתפרנס נותנין לו לשום הלואה וחוזרין
ונותנין לו לשום מתנה דברי רבי מאיר. וחכמים אומרים נותנין לו
לשום מתנה וחוזרין ונותנין לו לשום הלואה. לשום מתנה הא לא
שקיל? אמר רבא לפתוח לו לשום מתנה . . . ר"ש אומר . . . אומרים
לו הבא משכון וטול כדי שתזוח דעתו עליו.

The Sages taught: If an individual does not have suf-
ficient means of support and does not want to be sup-
ported from charity funds, the charities provide him
funds as a loan, and then they go back and give the
funds to him as a gift; this is the statement of Rabbi
Meir.

And the Rabbis say: They give him funds as a gift, and
then they go back and give the funds to him as a loan.

How can we give it as a gift—after all, he does not
want to take it as a gift? Rava said: [The Rabbis' in-
struction is] to begin discussions with him by offering
the assistance as a gift. If he refuses, the charities give
it to him as a loan, but they treat it as a gift and re-
frain from attempting to collect a debt...Rabbi Shimon
says...The charities say to him: Bring collateral and
take a loan, so that his mindset should be raised for
him, with the false impression that he is not receiving
a handout.

TEXT 9B

Rashi ad loc.

"שֶׁתָּזוּחַ דַּעְתּוֹ עָלָיו." יִגְבַּה לִבּוֹ לוֹמַר דַּעְתָּם לַחֲזוֹר וְלִגְבּוֹת הַיְמֵנִי הוֹאִיל וְתָבְעוּנִי מַשְׁכּוֹן אֵין זוֹ אֶלָּא הַלְוָאָה וְיִטּוֹל בְּלֹא בּוֹשֶׁת שֶׁיֹּאמַר אֵין לִי מַשְׁכּוֹן וְהֵם יֹאמְרוּ טוֹל בְּלֹא מַשְׁכּוֹן.

"So that his mindset should be raised for him." He will heartened and say to himself, "Surely they intend to collect the money from me. If they are bringing collateral, it must mean this is a loan." He will thus take the funds without shame, for he will say, "I do not have collateral," and they will reply, "Take the funds even without collateral."

The Value of Something Earned

TEXT 10

"The Best Compliment? Completing each Other"
By Chana Levitan (from chabad.org)

Take Lenny, one of the people in my relationship study, who told me about his earliest encounters with his wife. "I felt really centered around Carla. It felt great. Her serious, quiet side brought out a part of me that I always wanted to have. And she loved my crazy, outgoing personality. I loved to watch her come out of herself around me." Lenny got a glimpse into who he could really become—centered and grounded—and what his relationship with Carla could become. In other words, he realized (partially subconsciously) that their completion as a couple would also be a doorway—and a shortcut—to his own individual completion.

A few months after the wedding, however, Lenny started getting frustrated with Carla's reserved nature. "Now that we're married, it's so frustrating. She is so serious, and when we go out, she is really quiet. Why can't she just interact with people?" We can all relate to Lenny's annoyance. The energy flowed so easily in the beginning. Now it did not.

But the story is as follows: The completion we initially feel with our spouses is like a free gift to show us the potential of what we can have. Then, the training wheels are taken off; this is when every couple needs to put some effort in, to make that completion real.

If we want to succeed in anything, then we need to work at it. If we want to be a great athlete, we need to work out. If we want to be great doctors, we need to invest in years of study and practice. And if we want to attain the completion we experienced while we were dating—both on a personal level and on a relationship level—we need to put in some real effort.

We all have an independent part of ourselves that might struggle with this idea. On some level, we want to believe that we can become completed individuals on our own. Why should we need to get married to do this? Here's an analogy: Marriage is like a jam session. If you want to make great music with someone else, what's the prerequisite? To play solo. But if you can play solo, that doesn't mean that you can automatically jam. Only when you play with others do you realize where you're out of tune or rhythm.

In life, no matter how well we play solo, we will never see ourselves as we truly are (and therefore can never come into our true potential) until we can successfully jam with someone else. We spend a lot of time playing solo, but only when we get super close with someone—specifically in the lifelong, committed relationship of marriage—will we see and understand where we need fine-tuning in order to grow into the happiest, most loving versions of ourselves. Although other types of relationships assist us in this, only marriage—that lifelong commitment to one's partner—has the power to show us who we truly are and can become.

TEXT 11

The Lubavitcher Rebbe, Likutei Sichot, vol. 3, p. 1009

שטייט דער ביאור אויף דעם: ווען איז די השפעה אמיתית הטוב,
ווען דער מקבל באקומט זי פארדינטערהייט, ניט אומזיסט. בשעת
מען גיט עמעצן א מתנת חנם, אויף וועלכער יענער האט ניט
געהארעוועט, הייסט עס "נהמא דכסופא". און וויבאלד אז "טבע
הטוב להטיב" האט דער אויבערשטער געוואלט געבן אידן דעם
אמת'ן טוב, דעריבער האט ער איינגעשטעלט אז די השפעות זאלן
זיי באקומען דורך עבודה דוקא.

True divine kindness is when it is received through work, not for free. When a person is given a free gift, which he did not work for, it is "bread of shame." Because [G-d is the Essence of Goodness and] "it is the nature of Good to do good," G-d wanted to give the Jewish people true goodness, and therefore set that divine revelation come about specifically through toil.

Rabbi Menachem Mendel Schneerson
1902–1994

The towering Jewish leader of the 20th century, known as "the Lubavitcher Rebbe," or simply as "the Rebbe." Born in southern Ukraine, the Rebbe escaped Nazi-occupied Europe, arriving in the U.S. in June 1941. The Rebbe inspired and guided the revival of traditional Judaism after the European devastation, impacting virtually every Jewish community the world over. The Rebbe often emphasized that the performance of just one additional good deed could usher in the era of Mashiach. The Rebbe's scholarly talks and writings have been printed in more than 200 volumes.

Emulating G-d

If It Ain't Broken, Don't Fix It

TEXT 12

The Lubavitcher Rebbe, Likutei Sichot, vol. 15, p. 95

מ'קען ניט זאגן, אז דאס איז דערפאר וואס א מענטש בטבעו האט
תענוג (בעיקר) פון א זאך וואס ער באקומט דורך זיין הארעוואניע,
ע"ד מאמר רז"ל, אדם רוצה בקב שלו מט' קבים של חבירו—
וואָרום אָט די טבע גופא איז ניט קיין ענין הכרחי מצד עצמו, נאר
דער אויבערשטער האט עס אזוי מטביע געווען אין מענטשן; איז
הדרא קושיא לדוכתא; פארוואס האט דער אויבערשטער באשאפן
דעם מענטשן מיט א טבע צו האבן תענוג דוקא פוו זאכן וואס ער
באקומט דורך עמל ויגיעה—ענייני צער—און ניט פון מתנת חנם?

*We cannot answer [the question why G-d created the
world in a way that we must work hard] tis because a
person primarily enjoys the product of his own work,
as the Sages said, "A person prefers a kav of his own
produce to nine kav of another's produce." Ultimately,
this rule of human nature is not of inherent necessity,
but rather something that has been determined by
G-d; if so, the question stands: Why did G-d create
man with the nature to specifically enjoy the product
of his own labor—which involves difficulty—and not
something that is free?*

Being G-dly

TEXT 13

Maimonides, Sefer Hamitzvot Mitzvah 8

היא שצונו להדמות בו יתעלה כפי היכולת והוא אמרו והלכת
בדרכיו. וכבר נכפל זה הצווי ואמר ללכת בכל דרכיו ובא בפירוש
מה הקב"ה נקרא חנון אף אתה היה חנון מה הקב"ה נקרא רחום אף
אתה היה רחום מה הקב"ה נקרא חסיד אף אתה היה חסיד. וכבר
נכפל זה הענין בלשון אחר ואמר אחרי ה' תלכו ובא בפירוש שרצה
לומר ההדמות בפעולותיו הטובות והמדות הנכבדות שיתואר בהם
האל יתעלה על צד המשל. יתעלה על הכל עילוי רב.

The 8th mitzvah is that we are commanded to emulate G-d, blessed be He, to the best of our ability. The source of this commandment is G-d's statement (exalted be He), "And you shall walk in His paths." This commandment is repeated in the verse, "To walk in all His ways." This means, "Just as G-d is called merciful, so too, you must be merciful. Just as G-d is called kind, so too, you must be kind. Just as G-d is called righteous, so too, you must be righteous. Just as G-d is called pious, so too, you must be pious."

This commandment is also repeated in the verse, "Walk after G-d your Lord." This too means emulating the good deeds and fine attributes which are used to allegorically describe G-d (exalted be He), who is immeasurably exalted over everything.

Creative Creatures

TEXT 14

The Lubavitcher Rebbe, Likutei Sichot, vol. 15, p. 95

דער ביאור אין דעם: אמיתיות ותכלית הטוב איז, אז דער מענטש
זאל דערגרייכן (ניט נאר די העכסטע שלימות וואס איז דא אין גדר
הנבראים, נאר אויך) א מדריגה וואס אין איר ווערט ער, כביכול,
דומה, לבוראו, וע"ד לשון חז"ל, "שותף להקב"ה במעשה בראשית".
דעריבער האט דער אויבערשטער איינגעשטעלט דעם סדר
הבריאה, אז דער מענטש זאל זיינע באדערפענישן ניט באקומעז
מן המוכן, נאר דוקא דורך עמל ויגיעה, בכדי אז דורכדעם זאל ער
זיך אויפהויבן (ניט נאר צו דער שלימות פון א מקבל כדבעי — די
שלימות פון א נברא, נאר אויר) צו דער מדריגה פון א "משפיע"
(ומהווה)—דומה לבוראו, דורכדעם וואס דער מענטש הארעוועט
און שאפט בכח עצמו.

און דאס גופא איז דער טעם אויף דער טבע הנ"ל, אז א מענטש
האט ניט קיין תענוג פון זאכן וואס ער באקומט בחנם, נאר אדרבה,
ער שעמט זיר דערמיט —"נהמא דכסופא"—ווייל אין דעם אדם
איז מוטבע אז זיין תפקיד און שלימות איז צו זיין ניט נאר א ,מקבל",
נאר (אויר) א "משפיע", דומה לבוראו.

True goodness for a person is to attain not only the highest order of human perfection, but to also attain a level wherein one is similar, as it were, to his Creator, as the Sages said, "G-d's partner in creation."

Therefore, G-d embedded in our nature the need to procure our needs specifically through our own efforts, rather than achieve them automatically, so that one may rise not only to the perfection of a created being—something which is inherently a receiver—but also to the level of a "giver" (and creator)—similar to his own Creator, by working and producing with his own efforts.

This is the reason that, by nature, a person does not take pleasure in things he receives without effort, but rather finds them to be as "bread of shame," for embedded in a person's nature is the fact that his purpose and ultimate goal is not only to be a "receiver" but also a "giver," similar to his Creator.

7

Unlocking the Hair Lock

The Secret of the Upshernish

Dedicated to **Daniel Markson** in appreciation of his partnership in bringing
the light of Torah to communities around the globe.

PARSHAH OVERVIEW
Shoftim

Moses instructs the people of Israel to appoint judges and law enforcement officers in every city. "Justice, justice shall you pursue," he commands them, and you must administer it without corruption or favoritism. Crimes must be meticulously investigated and evidence thoroughly examined—a minimum of two credible witnesses is required for conviction and punishment.

In every generation, says Moses, there will be those entrusted with the task of interpreting and applying the laws of the Torah. "According to the law that they will teach you, and the judgment they will instruct you, you shall do; you shall not turn away from the thing that they say to you, to the right nor to the left."

Shoftim also includes the prohibitions against idolatry and sorcery; laws governing the appointment and behavior of a king; and guidelines for the creation of "cities of refuge" for the inadvertent murderer. Also set forth are many of the rules of war: the exemption from battle for one who has just built a home, planted a vineyard, married, or is "afraid and soft-hearted"; the requirement to offer terms of peace before attacking a city; and the prohibition against wanton destruction of something of value, exemplified by the law that forbids to cut down a fruit tree when laying siege (in this context the Torah makes the famous statement, "For man is a tree of the field").

The parshah *concludes with the law of the* eglah arufah—*the special procedure to be followed when a person is killed by an unknown murderer and his body is found in a field—which underscores the responsibility of the community and its leaders not only for what they do, but also for what they might have prevented from being done.*

First Shearings

The Mitzvah of the First-Shorn Wool

TEXT 1

Devarim (Deuteronomy) 18:1–5

לֹא יִהְיֶה לַכֹּהֲנִים הַלְוִיִּם כָּל שֵׁבֶט לֵוִי חֵלֶק וְנַחֲלָה עִם יִשְׂרָאֵל אִשֵּׁי ה'
וְנַחֲלָתוֹ יֹאכֵלוּן. וְנַחֲלָה לֹא יִהְיֶה לּוֹ בְּקֶרֶב אֶחָיו ה' הוּא נַחֲלָתוֹ כַּאֲשֶׁר
דִּבֶּר לוֹ.
וְזֶה יִהְיֶה מִשְׁפַּט הַכֹּהֲנִים מֵאֵת הָעָם מֵאֵת זֹבְחֵי הַזֶּבַח אִם שׁוֹר אִם
שֶׂה וְנָתַן לַכֹּהֵן הַזְּרֹעַ וְהַלְּחָיַיִם וְהַקֵּבָה. רֵאשִׁית דְּגָנְךָ תִּירֹשְׁךָ וְיִצְהָרֶךָ
וְרֵאשִׁית גֵּז צֹאנְךָ תִּתֶּן לּוֹ.
כִּי בוֹ בָּחַר ה' אֱלֹקֶיךָ מִכָּל שְׁבָטֶיךָ לַעֲמֹד לְשָׁרֵת בְּשֵׁם ה' הוּא וּבָנָיו
כָּל הַיָּמִים.

The levitic kohanim, the entire tribe of Levi, shall have no portion or inheritance with Israel; G-d's fire offerings and His inheritance they shall eat. But he shall have no inheritance among his brothers; G-d is his inheritance, as He spoke to him.

And this shall be the kohanim's due from the people, from those who perform a slaughter, be it an ox or a sheep, he shall give the kohen the foreleg, the jaws, and the maw.

The first of your grain, your wine, and your oil, and the first of the fleece of your sheep you shall give him.

TEXT 2

Rabbi Aharon Halevi of Barcelona, Sefer HaChinuch 508

משרשי המצוה . . . והכהנים כמו כן שהם המשרתים תמיד פני
השם ואין להם נחלה בקרקעות, ולא בביזה, זכה להם השם יתברך
כל צורך מחיתם על ידי אחיהם.

והנה נתן להם התרומה ומעשר מן המעשר, שהם לחמם וייִנם,
ומתנות בהמה, שהם זרוע ולחיים וקבה, וחלקם בקדשי מקדש,
שיש להם בשר די ספקם, ועדיין חסר להם מלבוש, זכה להם
ראשית הגז למלבושיהם, ועוד זכה להם שדה אחזה, וגזל הגר,
והחרמים, ופדיון בכורות, לשאר הוצאות וצרכים שהאדם צריך.

**Rabbi Aharon Halevi
of Barcelona**
(Re'ah)
1235–1290

Born in Gerona, Spain. Rabbi,
talmudist, and authority on
Jewish law. Rabbi Aharon
studied under Nachmanides
and under his father,
Rabbi Yosef Halevi, and
corresponded with the leading
talmudic scholars of his
generation. His explanations
on the Rashba's halachic
code, *Torat Habayit*, entitled
Bedek Habayit, are integral
in the formation of Jewish
law. Rabbi Aharon was
considered by some to be the
anonymous author of *Sefer
Hachinuch*, a compendium
of the 613 commandments.

*The reason for the mitzvah of giving the first shearing
to the kohen… Because the priests serve constantly in
front of G-d and have no share in land or bounty, G-d
made sure they were able to acquire all their worldly
needs through their brethren, the Israelites.*

*G-d set aside for the kohen the priestly tithe and the
tithe of the tithe, the source of their bread and wine,
and the animal gifts of foreleg, jaw, and maw, as well
as parts from the Temple sacrifices, so they would not
want for meat. However, the priests would still lack
clothing. Thus, G-d provided for them the first shearing, from which they could create clothes.*

*G-d also set aside for them the field of possession,
the recovered theft of the convert who has died, the
expropriations and the money from redeeming the*

first-borns, so they would have money for all other necessary expenses.

A Modern-Day First Shearing

TEXT 3

The Lubavitcher Rebbe, Igrot Kodesh, vol. 21, p. 95

Rabbi Menachem Mendel Schneerson
1902–1994

The towering Jewish leader of the 20th century, known as "the Lubavitcher Rebbe," or simply as "the Rebbe." Born in southern Ukraine, the Rebbe escaped Nazi-occupied Europe, arriving in the U.S. in June 1941. The Rebbe inspired and guided the revival of traditional Judaism after the European devastation, impacting virtually every Jewish community the world over. The Rebbe often emphasized that the performance of just one additional good deed could usher in the era of Mashiach. The Rebbe's scholarly talks and writings have been printed in more than 200 volumes.

זה הוא יום "ראשית הגז" של בנו שי', הנני לאחל אשר כל ברכות כבוד קדושת מורי וחמי אדמו"ר שליט"א יקויימו במילואן, והוא וביתו יחיו יגדלו את בנם לתורה חופה ומעשים טובים.

This is the day of the "first shearing" of your son, may he live. May the blessings of the Previous Rebbe be utterly fulfilled, and you and your household raise your son to Torah, the marriage canopy, and good deeds!

TEXT 4

Rabbi Mordechai Lipitz, Mata'amim, "Hair", 1

טעם למנהג שאין מגלחין השערות מתינוק עד שמתחיל לדבר:
משום דאיתא בגמרא דאיתא תינוק שמתחיל לדבר אביו מלמדו תורה
מהו "תורה צוה לנו משה וגו'", ועל כן הוא מקדישו לשמים, וכתיב
"ראשית גז צאנך תתן לו", וישראל קרויין צאן. ועל כן כשמתחיל
לדבר ומכניסו לקדושה נוטל ממנו שערותיו ונותן דמיו לשמים.

A reason for the custom of not cutting a boy's hair until he begins to speak: The Talmud states that a father is obligated to teach his child Torah when the child begins to speak. What does he teach? The verse "The Torah was commanded to us by Moses, an inheritance for the congregation of Jacob."

Thus, at the age the boy can begin to speak he is dedicated to G-d in sanctity, as is written, "The first shearing of your sheep give to Him." Just as the sheep's wool is set aside for holy purposes and given to the kohen, so too are the children of Israel allegorically called sheep. Therefore, when a boy begins to speak and is brought into the holy world of Torah, we shear his hair and dedicate its worth to heaven.

Early Sources

TEXT 5

Rabbi Yitzchak Luria, the Arizal, Shaar HaKavanot,
Inyan Pesach u'Sefirat Ha'Omer, Sermon 12

Rabbi Yitzchak Luria
1534–1572
Known by the acronym
"Arizal," or simply "the Ari."
Founder of the Lurianic
school of Kabbalah. Born in
Jerusalem; raised in Egypt;
died in Safed. Rabbi Luria
studied Talmud under Rabbi
Betzalel Ashkenazi, compiler
of the *Shitah Mekubetzet*.
Despite his youth, he was
accepted among the rabbinic
elite of Safed. The Ari never
recorded his teachings; they
were collected and transcribed
by his disciples. His leading
disciple, Rabbi Chaim Vital,
is generally considered the
most authoritative recorder
of the Arizal's teachings.

ענין מנהג שנהגו ישראל ללכת ביום ל"ג לעומר על קברי רשב"י
ורבי אלעזר בנו אשר קבורים בעיר מירון כנודע ואוכלים ושותים
ושמחים שם.

אני ראיתי למורי ז"ל שהלך לשם פעם אחד ביום ל"ג לעומר, הוא
וכל אנשי ביתו, וישב שם שלשה ימים ראשונים של השבוע ההוא,
וזה היה פעם הא' שבא ממצרים. אבל אין אני יודע אם אז היה בקי
ויודע בחכמה הזו הנפלאה שהשיג אחר כך.

וההר"ר יונתן שאגי"ש העיד לי שבשנה הא' קודם שהלכתי אני אצלו
ללמוד עם מורי ז"ל שהוליך את בנו הקטן שם עם כל אנשי ביתו
ושם גילחו את ראשו כמנהג הידוע ועשה שם יום משתה ושמחה.

*There is a custom for Jews to travel on Lag Ba'Omer
to the graves of Rabbi Shimon bar Yochai and Rabbi
Elazar his son, who are buried in the town of Meron,
and to eat, drink, and celebrate there.*

*I saw my teacher, the Ari of blessed memory, travel
there once on Lag Ba'Omer, he and his entire household, and stay there for the first three days of the week,
when he first arrived from Egypt. I do not, however,
know if he had already at that time mastered the
wondrous wisdom he came to grasp afterward.*

Rabbi Yonatan Shaagish told me that the year before I came to study under him the Arizal took his young son there with his entire household and cut his son's hair according to the well-known custom, in a day of feasting and rejoicing.

TEXT 6

Rabbi Chanoch Ehrentreu, Shirei Minchah, 10:5

בשנה זו זכיתי להיות בל"ג בעומר על ציון המצויינת קודש הקדשים דרשב"י זי"ע במירון, וראיתי שמה בעיני כל הלילה עד חצות היום ערב שבת קודש השמחה והריקודים בתופים ובמחולות, ממש כשמחת בית השואבה.

וכאור בוקר באו חסידים ואנשי מעשה לבוש בבגדי שבת עם בניהם הקטנים, ושם גיזזו את ראשם, ומכבדים את כל אחד ואחד שיגלח קצת את בנו ולברכו שיזכה לגדלו שיהיה תלמיד חכם ירא שמים ומיני מזונות, ומברכים 'לחיים' לאבי הקטנים שיגדלם לתורה ויראת שמים.

והאבות לקחו את בנים הקטנים על כתיפיו וכך מרקדים ומזמרים עמהם שעות הרבה.

This year, I merited to spend Lag Ba'Omer at the holy of holies, the gravesite of Rabbi Shimon bar Yochai at Meron. I saw there with my own eyes the dancing and celebration from Thursday evening until midday Friday, truly the same as the water-drawing celebration of the Temple.

In the light of morning, Chasidim and men of great deeds came dressed in their Shabbat finery with their small sons and cut their hair, and honored all present with the opportunity to shear a little hair from their child and bless him to grow into a Torah scholar with the fear of heaven. They provided refreshments and we blessed "l'chaim!" to the fathers that their sons should grow to Torah and fear of heaven.

The fathers then took their sons on their shoulders and danced and sang for many hours.

TEXT 7

Achiasaf, Warsaw 1904, #14

ירדנו ובאנו אל תוך "המדרש". ולפני מראה מפליא: בתוך הרעש וההמולה של ההמון אשר בבית מתאספים יהודים שונים, ועל זרועותיהם ילדים קטנים בני שלש הלבושים מכנסיים יפים וקפוטות קטנות ונקיות, ועל ראשיהם מצנפות עגולות מוזהבות בשפתן העשויות לכבוד ההילולא והתספורת. מתחת למצנפת הילדים נשקף סבך של שערות הראש והפיאות בלתי מסורקות.

האבות מחלקים יין מגדנות וממתקים לכל עובר. ויהודי אחד מגבאי הבית ניגש ובידו מספריים ובזהירות בדברי פיוס לילד הוא מתחיל לגזוז את קצות פיאותיו.

הילד מרוב פחד ותמהון מתפרץ בבכי גדול. השערות נסתפרו ונפלו
ארצה, וככלות הספר את עבודתו בירך את האב לאמור: 'יעזור לך
ה' ובנך יהיה יהודי כשר ועובד את השם יתברך'.

We descended and arrived at the "study hall," and
before me was a wondrous sight:

Among the loud and tumultuous masses gathered in the
building were various Jews with their three-year-old
sons in their arms. The boys were dressed in fine pants
and small, clean coats, and on their heads were round
gilded caps made in honor of the occasion, the haircut.
Beneath their caps were tangles of unshorn hair.

The fathers handed out wine and sweets to all pass-
ersby. One Jew, among the caretakers of the building,
arrived with scissors. Carefully, and with calming
words to the child, he began to shear the edge of a
child's hair.

The child cried out from fear and shock. The hair fell
to the ground, and when the barber finished his work,
he blessed the father, saying: "G-d should help you
and your son should be a kosher Jew who serves the
blessed G-d."

'Educate the child...'

TEXT 8

Text of the Rebbe's Letter for Upsherenish

במענה על ההודעה אודות יום הולדת השלישי של בנם .. שי'
הנה מועתק לקמן חלק ממכתב מו"ח אדמו"ר זצוקללה"ה נבג"מ
זי"ע בנוגע למנהגי ישראל בזה, ויהי רצון מהשי"ת שיגדלו ביחד עם
זוגתו תחי' לתורה ולחופה ולמעשים טובים מתוך הרחבה.
בברכה מ. שניאורסאהן
וזה לשון כ"ק מו"ח אדמו"ר.
... ובדבר גזיזת השערות - אפשערעניש - הוא דבר גדול במנהג
ישראל ועיקרו הוא בהחינוך דהשארת פיאות הראש, ומיום הגזיזה
והנחת הפיאות של הראש, נהגו להדר להרגיל את התינוק בענין
נשיאת טלית קטן וברכות השחר וברכת המזון וקריאת שמע
שעל המטה.
והשם יתברך יהיה בעזרם שיגדלוהו לתורה ולחופה ולמעשים
טובים מתוך פרנסה בהרחבה ובמנוחת הדעת בגשמיות וברוחניות.

Greetings and blessings,

*In response to the notification of your son's, _____,
upcoming third birthday, I am attaching an excerpt
from a letter from my revered father-in-law and
teacher, the Rebbe, with regard to this Jewish custom.
May it be G-d's will that you and your wife raise him
[and enable him] to attain Torah, marriage, and good
deeds amidst prosperity.*

With blessing,

[The Rebbe's signature]

This is the quote from my revered father-in-law and teacher, the Rebbe:

With regard to [a child's first] haircut, the upsheren-ish*: It is a matter of great [significance] among the customs of the Jewish people. The idea behind it is to train [the child to] leave* peyot *[sidelocks]. From the day of the haircut [when] the* peyot *are left it is customary to carefully train the child to wear a* tallit katan *and to recite the morning blessings, the Grace after Meals, and the Shema before retiring.*

May G-d assist you to raise your child [and enable him] to attain Torah, marriage, and good deeds amidst abundant sustenance and peace of mind in both material and spiritual matters.

The Meaning of the Custom

To Leave the Sidelocks Untouched

TEXT 9

Vayikra (Leviticus) 19:27

לֹא תַקִּפוּ פְּאַת רֹאשְׁכֶם וְלֹא תַשְׁחִית אֵת פְּאַת זְקָנֶךָ׃

You shall not round off the corner (pe'at) of your head, and you shall not destroy the edge of your beard.

TEXT 10

Shulchan Aruch, Yoreh Dei'ah 181: 9

פאות הראש הם שתים סוף הראש הוא מקום חיבורו ללחי
מימין ומשמאל.

בין שגילח הפאות בלבד בין שגילח כל הראש עם הפאות חייב.

שיעור הפאה מכנגד שער שעל פדחתו ועד למטה מן האוזן מקום
שהלחי התחתון יוצא ומתפרד שם וכל רוחב מקום זה לא תגע
בו יד.

Rabbi Yosef Caro
(Maran, *Beit Yosef*)
1488–1575

Halachic authority and author.
Rabbi Caro was born in Spain,
but was forced to flee during
the expulsion in 1492 and
eventually settled in Safed,
Israel. He authored many
works including the *Beit Yosef*,
Kesef Mishneh, and a mystical
work, *Magid Meisharim*.
Rabbi Caro's magnum opus,
the Shulchan Aruch (Code
of Jewish Law), has been
universally accepted as the
basis for modern Jewish law.

The "corner of the head," the peyos, *are the two points on the head where the scalp meets the jaw on the left and right side.*

Whether one shaves only the peyos, *or the entire head including the* peyos, *one has transgressed the prohibition.*

The extent of the sidelock is from parallel to the hairline on the forehead up to below the ear, where the jaw emerges and separates from the head. The entire breadth of that place must be left untouched.

TEXT 11

Rabbi Yonah Navon, Responsa Nechpah Bakesef, vol. 2 p. 18

מעשה שהיה שבחול המועד של סוכות משנת אשר"י [=תקי"א]
העם גלחו תגלחת ראשונה לקטן עם ספר ישראל בתופים
ובמחולות בפרהסיא כמו שנוהגים לעשות בשביל חיבוב מצות
הפאה שמניחים לו.
והיו מערערים בדבר שאין ראוי לעשות כן על ידי ספר ישראל
בחול המועד כו'.

A true story: On Chol HaMoed Sukkot of the year 5511 (1751), the community gave a boy his first haircut with a Jewish barber, in public, with drumming and dancing, as is the custom for honoring the leaving over of the peyot.

There were those who questioned this behavior, wondering whether it was proper to do with a Jewish barber on Chol HaMoed.

Looking Jewish

TEXT 12

Midrash Eichah Rabah 2:17

"בתולת בת ציון"—בנים המצוייניין במילה ובתגלחת [שנאסרו בהקפת הראש ובהשחתת הזקן, מתנות כהונה] ובציצית.

"The maiden of Zion"—Her sons are marked by circumcision, by their hairstyle (namely, beard and peyot—Matnot Kehunah), and by their tzitzit.

Eichah Rabah

A Midrashic text on the Book of Lamentations, produced by the sages of the Talmud in the Land of Israel. Its language closely resembles that of the Jerusalem Talmud. It was first printed in Pesaro, Italy, in 1519, together with four other midrashic works on the other four *megilot*.

TEXT 13

Olam Asiyah, vol. 1 p. 32b

וראשון לראשונה יסיתהו להעביר מעל פניו אותות היהדות (יודען שיהלט) דהיינו להסיר פאות הראש והזקן במספרים שהם אות שבהם ניכר אשר הוא יהודי.

First things first, the force of evil will tempt him to remove from his face his Jewish appearance, that is, to remove his peyot *and beard, the signs by which he is externally recognized as a Jew, with scissors.*

TEXT 14

Mata'amim, Ibid.

טעם למנהג שאין מגלחין השערות מתינוק עד שמתחיל לדבר . . .
ואז גם כן מחנכו למצות ומשייר לו פאות ועושהו יהודי שיהיה ניכר
לכל שהוא תינוק יהודי. שמעתי.

The reason for the custom not to cut a boy's hair until he begins to speak… I have heard that this is also the time when we educate him about the mitzvot, and leave him peyot, *which make him recognizable in the eyes of the world as a Jewish child.*

Sidelocks of Faith

TEXT 15

Rabbi Aharon Halevi of Barcelona, Sefer HaChinuch, Mitzvah 251

שלא להקיף פאתי הראש, שנאמר [ויקרא י״ט, כ״ז] לא תקיפו פאת
ראשכם, ופירשו זכרונם לברכה שהענין הוא שאסור לישראל לגלח
ולהשוות שערות ראשו לאחורי אזניו ולפדחתו, כמו שעושים גם
היום עובדי עבודה זרה וכומריהם . . .

משרשי המצוה, כדי להרחיק ממנו ולהשכיח מבין עינינו ומכל
מעשינו כל ענין עבודה זרה וכל הנעשה בשבילה, ובאה האזהרה
מפורשת בדבר שיעשו לה בני אדם בגופותם, מפני שהיא למזכרת
עוון תמיד אחר שהיא דבר קבוע בגוף.

Sefer Hachinuch
A work on the biblical
commandments. Four aspects
of every mitzvah are discussed
in this work: the definition of
the mitzvah; ethical lessons
that can be deduced from
the mitzvah; basic laws
pertaining to the observance
of the mitzvah; and who is
obligated to perform the
mitzvah, and when. The work
was composed in the 13th
century by an anonymous
author who refers to himself
as "the Levite of Barcelona."
It has been widely thought
that this referred to Rabbi
Aharon Halevi of Barcelona
(Re'ah); however, this view
has been contested.

*To not round off the corner of the head, as it is stated,
"You shall not round off the corner of your head." The
Sages explain that a Jew is not allowed to shave and
style his hair similar to the idolaters and their priests
of today...*

*A reason for this commandment is to distance ourselves
from any matter of idolatry and anything that is done
for its sake—to make it forgotten from between our
eyes and from all of our actions. The warning comes
explicitly about a thing that people do on their bodies,
since it is "a perpetual reminder of iniquity," as it is
something that is fixed in the body.*

TEXT 16

Rabbi Moshe Sofer, Drashot Chatam Sofer, vol. 2, p. 319

Rabbi Moshe Sofer
(*Chatam Sofer*)
1762–1839

A leading rabbinical authority
of the 19th century. Born
in Frankfurt am Main,
Chatam Sofer ultimately
accepted the rabbinate of
Pressburg (now Bratislava),
Slovakia. Serving as rabbi
and head of the yeshiva
that he established, Rabbi
Sofer maintained a strong
traditionalist perspective,
opposing deviation from
Jewish tradition. *Chatam Sofer*
is the title of his collection
of halachic responsa and his
commentary to the Talmud.

אבל הנראה לפי עניות דעתי לפי מה שכתוב במורה טעם לאסור
השחתת פאה משום שהיה חוק לכומרים.
והנה אין אנו צריכים לטעמו כי תורה חתומה נתנה ואנו מקבלים
מצות כאשר ציונו ה' אלקינו. אך מכל מקום צריך לתת טעם
להשוטים הללו מה ראו לעשות כן לעבודה זרה ומה צורך יש בה?
ויראה כי דבר פלא כי עובדי פסילים עושים כל התחבולות לעשות
פסילים בתמונת אדם וכל מעשיהם בתחבולות וחכמות אך לעשות
לו שער זה אי אפשר בשום אופן בעולם אם לא ידביקו בו שער
מאדם אחר אבל להצמיח לו שער מיניה מקשה אחת זה אי אפשר.
ועל כן לכבוד פסיליהם עושים האמורים ההפך שמגלחים שעריהם
ופאותיהם לגמרי ויתדמו המה לפסיליהם.

I would like to suggest a reason for the ban on cutting the peyot, *based on what Rambam writes in Guide for the Perplexed that the logic is that such fashion was common among idolatrous priests.*

Now, we do not need to find a reason for any of the Torah's commandments, inasmuch as the Torah is a sealed treasure and we follow it purely because G-d commanded us so. However, we must still explain the thought process of the foolish idolatrous priests—why did they shave their entire heads? What need was there for that?

Observe the astonishing line of reasoning: Those who worshipped graven images concocted all sorts of methods to makes their idols look like human beings. They were successful in many ways, but they were entirely unable to recreate the true appearance of hair on their idols. They were only able to attach shorn human hair to their idols; to actually grow new hair from the idol is simply impossible.

So, in order to honor their idols, the idolatrous priests took the opposite approach: They shaved their own heads entirely, including the peyot area, to appear visibly similar to their idols.

Grow Up!

A Psychological Device

TEXT 17

Rabbi Isaac Schwei, Kitvei R'Izik, vol. 1, pp. 272ff.

Rabbi Isaac Schwei
1932–1988

A respected and influential figure in Chabad, Rabbi Schwei was born in Finland and was forced into hiding during the tumultuous years of WWII. After experiencing much success in the underground Chabad yeshiva system in the USSR, Rabbi Schwei eventually escaped the Iron Curtain and made his way to Montreal where he served as a rabbi, rosh yeshivah, and other important positions in the city. His books were published posthumously under direction from the Lubavitcher Rebbe.

ולהסביר הענין לבעלי הבית, "אויף א בעה"ב'טישן אופן", יש לומר כי מאחר שזהו פשוט—ככל אריכות ההסבר הנ"ל—שבהגיע התינוק לשלש אז הרי זה תקופה חשובה להרגילו בכמה עניני מצות, והיינו על פי הנאמר באברהם אבינו עליו השלום שבן שלש הכיר את בוראו, כן ראוי לנהוג אצל כל ילד וילד שבהגיעו לשלש להוסיף במידה מסויימת כמה וכמה ענינים, לימוד אותיות התורה וכו' וכו'.

אשר לכן, כיון שאנו רוצים שהתינוק ירגיש את זה, הנה צריכים שיהא באופן אשר לפי קוטן הבנתו ידע ויבחין כי נשתנה עכשיו ונעשה לבן שלש!

אשר אם כן הדבר אצל גדולים בשנים שיש צורך בענין החינוך כשנכנסים לשרת וכו' בכהונה וכן בכל דבר ודבר והדברים ידועים, אם כן על אחת כמה וכמה שכן צריך לנהוג בתינוק לעשות מזה דבר גדול, והדבר הכי מרשים והכי מתאים הוא להבליט ולהראות לו לפי ערכו אשר עד עכשיו היה תינוק ומעכשיו הוא נתגדל ויצא מגדר הזה.

ואיך לעשות דבר זה?

הרי דרך הכי טוב הוא על ידי שעד אז הולך בשערות ארוכות, וככל התינוקות, ועכשיו גוזזים שערותיו, וממילא מרגיש "שאינו עוד תינוק" כמו שהיה עד עכשיו, ומסייע זה לחנכו בכמה וכמה עניני חינוך, שאומרים לו עכשיו אתה צריך לעשות זה וזה וכו' אינך עוד תינוק וכו', או שלתינוק וילד כזה כמו אתה אין יאות לא לומר

> ברכה כו' כיון שאתה אינך תינוק כמו הפעוט ההוא וכו'—דברים המתקבלים היטב על לבו של תינוק ומתיישבים בדעתו ובהבנתו לפי ערכו.

To explain the matter in a straightforward way, so that even a pragmatist will understand it:

When a child reaches three years old, it is a period in their life when it is vital to habituate them to performing mitzvos. That is, just as our father, Abraham, recognized his Creator at three years old, so too it is fitting to add to every child's Torah education when they reach the age of three.

Inasmuch as we want the child to feel the importance of these new steps in his education, we must do it in a way that, even according to his small understanding, he realizes something has changed; he has reached the remarkable age of three years old!

We make a big deal even when it comes to older children (e.g., when they reach an age that they can serve as a kohen in the Temple, etc.); certainly we should do so with a small child. We must make a "big deal" out of this milestone in their lives, something that will leave an impression and demonstrate to them that until now they were babies not yet learning mitzvot, and now they have matured and left that category.

How do we accomplish this?

The best way is to take their hair, which has grown long until now like all their young friends, and cut it off, so that the child will come to realize that he "is no longer a baby." This, in turn, helps with several aspects of his education, in which we may now tell him, "You need to do such and such; you aren't a baby anymore," or "For a big child like you it's not proper not to say this blessing, you're not a baby like that toddler," etc.

These words will be accepted by the child and understood at his level.

The Kabbalah of Peyos

TEXT 18

Rabbi Yitzchak Luria, the Arizal, Sefer Taamei HaMitzvot, Kedoshim, The Prohibition of Shaving the Peyot

Rabbi Yitzchak Luria
1534–1572
Known by the acronym "Arizal," or simply "the Ari." Founder of the Lurianic school of kabbalah. Born in Jerusalem; raised in Egypt; died in Safed. Rabbi Luria studied Talmud under Rabbi Betzalel Ashkenazi, compiler of the *Shitah Mekubetzet*. Despite his youth, he was accepted among the rabbinic elite of Safed. The Ari never recorded his teachings; they were collected and transcribed by his disciples. His leading disciple, Rabbi Chaim Vital, is generally considered the most authoritative recorder of the Arizal's teachings.

בכל פעם שעושה מצוה אינו מספיק לו במה שעושה אותה אלא שיכוין בעשייתה לקיים מצות בוראו שצוהו בכך.

ונדבר במצות הפאה כשהוא מסתפר יכוין שאינו מניח לשחת לו פאת הראש מב' צדדיו וגם פאת הזקן.

. . וראוי לאדם לכוין כשמספר ראשו שהוא דוגמת ז"א ומסלק כל הגבורות דדינים ממנו . . ואמנם כבר ידעת כי הראש כלול מי"ס והמלכות שבו הוא סוד פאת הראש, לכן פאה גימטריא אלקים, ולעולם פאה הוא במלכות.

ואמנם אין קיום לעולם כי אם על ידי הדינים, ואין ראוי לסלקם לגמרי, לכן בחינת מלכות לבד אנו צריכים להניח וזו בריש דז"א.

Every time one fulfills a Divine commandment, one should not be satisfied with action alone but should perform it with the correct intention to fulfill the commandment his Creator has given him.

In the case of peyot, *while the hair is being cut, one ought to turn their mind to the fact that they do not have permission to cut their* peyot *on each side, nor to cut the corners of their beard…*

A person should realize when their hair is cut that their head is like Ze'ir Anpin, the Divine emotive qualities, and that all the severities of their judgments are being removed… However, it is known that the head is comprised of all ten Divine Sefirot, or modes of Divine expression, and the Malchut, the majesty of the head, is at the peyot. Therefore, the Hebrew word "pei'ah," the singular form of peyot, *has the same numerical value of "Elokim," the Divine name associated with Malchut.*

However, the world is only sustained by severity, and they should not be entirely removed, and therefore in Malchut alone we must leave over some of the severities, at the reisha, or head, of Ze'ir Anpin.

The Root of the Hair

TEXT 19

Rabbi Dov Ber of Lubavitch, Maamare'i Admur Ha'emtza'i, Devarim, vol. 3, p. 948

Rabbi Dovber of Lubavitch
(Miteler Rebbe)
1773–1827

Rabbi Dovber was the eldest son of and successor to Rabbi Shne'ur Zalman of Liadi and greatly expanded upon and developed his father's groundbreaking teachings. He was the first Chabad rebbe to live in the village of Lubavitch. Dedicated to the welfare of Russian Jewry, at that time confined to the Pale of Settlement, he established Jewish agricultural colonies. His most notable works on Chasidic thought include *Shaar Hayichud*, *Torat Chayim*, and *Imrei Binah*.

דכל שערה עניינה בחינת המשכה מצומצמת בבחינת דילוג הערך דוקא, כמו שמורה ציור אות הוי"ו שהולך בצמצום ודקות בראשו יו"ד והולך ונמשך בקוצר ודקות מאוד כו'.

וכך הראש ומקור דשערה הוא יניקות שרשה בגומא א' והולכת ונמשכת בחיות מועט מצומצום מאוד, שאם יחתוך אינו מרגיש כאב כלל, רק בהמשיך אותה ירגיש בשרש יניקתה איזה הרגש כאב מעט. והוא להיות כי יניקות החיות שנמשך בשערות הוא מבחינת מותרי הלחלוחית שבמוחין עצמם.

All hair is derived from a diluted and limited G-dly expression that is incomparably lower than its source. It is like the letter vav, which descends down the page narrowly, its head the mere point of a yud, and never expanding into a broad letter.

So too with hair, its head and source is where its root is sustained within a single pore, and it grows outward with an extremely limited and diluted life force. It is so limited, that if the hair is cut one feels no pain at all. One only feels pains if the hair is pulled—because there is more life in the root than in the rest of the strand.

This is all because the sustenance drawn into the hair only derives from the "moisture of the brain rather than the brains themselves.

Good Within Limits

TEXT 20

Midrash Bereishit Rabah 12:15

"ביום עשות ה' אלקים ארץ ושמים".

משל למלך שהיו לו כוסות ריקים, אמר המלך אם אני נותן לתוכן חמין הם מתבקעין, צונן הם מקריסין. ומה עשה המלך? ערב חמין בצונן ונתן בהם ועמדו.

כך אמר הקדוש ברוך הוא: אם בורא אני את העולם במדת הרחמים, הוי חטייה סגיאין. במדת הדין היאך העולם יכול לעמוד? אלא, הרי אני בורא אותו במדת הדין ובמדת הרחמים, והלואי יעמוד.

Bereishit Rabah

An early rabbinic commentary on the Book of Genesis. This Midrash bears the name of Rabbi Oshiya Rabah (Rabbi Oshiya "the Great"), whose teaching opens this work. This Midrash provides textual exegeses and stories, expounds upon the biblical narrative, and develops and illustrates moral principles. Produced by the sages of the Talmud in the Land of Israel, its use of Aramaic closely resembles that of the Jerusalem Talmud. It was first printed in Constantinople in 1512 together with four other Midrashic works on the other four books of the Pentateuch.

"On the day G-D Elokim created heaven and earth."

This is analogous to a king who possessed empty cups. The king said, "If I place hot drinks in them, they will shatter. If I put cold drink in them, they will congeal." What did the king do? He mixed hot and cold and poured it into the cups, and the mixture was stable.

So said the Holy One, blessed be He: "If I create the world only with mercy, then it would be dominated by transgressors. If I create the world only with severity, how could the world survive? Rather, I will create it with a combination of kindness and severity, and I hope it will survive."

8

KI TETZEI

Mazal Tov, Mazal Tov!

Every Day Your Wedding Day

*Dedicated in merit of **Avraham Yaakov** ben **Ariella** and **Esther** bat **Ariella**. They should merit to live a life in constant awareness of Hashem and hiskashrus to the Rebbe!*

PARSHAH OVERVIEW
Ki Tetzei

Seventy-four of the Torah's 613 commandments (mitzvot) are in the parshah of Ki Teitzei. These include the laws of the beautiful captive, the inheritance rights of the firstborn, the wayward and rebellious son, burial and dignity of the dead, returning a lost object, sending away the mother bird before taking her young, the duty to erect a safety fence around the roof of one's home, and the various forms of kilayim (forbidden plant and animal hybrids).

Also recounted are the judicial procedures and penalties for adultery, for the rape or seduction of an unmarried girl, and for a husband who falsely accuses his wife of infidelity. The following cannot marry a person of Jewish lineage: a mamzer (someone born from an adulterous or incestuous relationship); a male of Moabite or Ammonite descent; a first- or second-generation Edomite or Egyptian.

Our Parshah also includes laws governing the purity of the military camp; the prohibition against turning in an escaped slave; the duty to pay a worker on time, and to allow anyone working for you—man or animal—to "eat on the job"; the proper treatment of a debtor, and the prohibition against charging interest on a loan; the laws of divorce (from which are also derived many of the laws of marriage); the penalty of thirty-nine lashes for transgression of a Torah prohibition; and the procedures for yibbum *("levirate marriage") of the wife of a deceased childless brother, or* chalitzah *("removing of the shoe") in the case that the brother-in-law does not wish to marry her.*

Ki Teitzei concludes with the obligation to remember "what Amalek did to you on the road, on your way out of Egypt."

Marriage in the Torah

A Match Made in Ikea

TEXT 1

Bereishit (Genesis) 2:21–24

וַיַּפֵּל ה' אֱלֹקִים תַּרְדֵּמָה עַל הָאָדָם וַיִּישָׁן וַיִּקַּח אַחַת מִצַּלְעֹתָיו וַיִּסְגֹּר בָּשָׂר תַּחְתֶּנָּה:

וַיִּבֶן ה' אֱלֹקִים אֶת הַצֵּלָע אֲשֶׁר לָקַח מִן הָאָדָם לְאִשָּׁה וַיְבִאֶהָ אֶל הָאָדָם:

וַיֹּאמֶר הָאָדָם זֹאת הַפַּעַם עֶצֶם מֵעֲצָמַי וּבָשָׂר מִבְּשָׂרִי לְזֹאת יִקָּרֵא אִשָּׁה כִּי מֵאִישׁ לֻקֳחָה זֹּאת:

עַל כֵּן יַעֲזָב אִישׁ אֶת אָבִיו וְאֶת אִמּוֹ וְדָבַק בְּאִשְׁתּוֹ וְהָיוּ לְבָשָׂר אֶחָד:

And the Lord G-d caused a deep sleep to fall upon man, and he slept, and He took one of his sides, and He closed the flesh in its place.

And the Lord G-d built the side that He had taken from man into a woman, and He brought her to man.

And man said, "this time, it is bone of my bones and flesh of my flesh. This one shall be called "ishah" (woman) because this one was taken from "ish" (man).

Therefore, a man shall leave his father and his mother and cleave to his wife, and they shall become one flesh.

Get Serious, or Stay Away

TEXT 2

Devarim (Deuteronomy) 22:13–21

כִּי יִקַּח אִישׁ אִשָּׁה וּבָא אֵלֶיהָ וּשְׂנֵאָהּ:
וְשָׂם לָהּ עֲלִילֹת דְּבָרִים וְהוֹצִא עָלֶיהָ שֵׁם רָע וְאָמַר אֶת הָאִשָּׁה הַזֹּאת
לָקַחְתִּי וָאֶקְרַב אֵלֶיהָ וְלֹא מָצָאתִי לָהּ בְּתוּלִים: . . .
וְאִם אֱמֶת הָיָה הַדָּבָר הַזֶּה לֹא נִמְצְאוּ בְתוּלִים לַנַּעֲרָ:
וְהוֹצִיאוּ אֶת הַנַּעֲרָ אֶל פֶּתַח בֵּית אָבִיהָ וּסְקָלוּהָ אַנְשֵׁי עִירָהּ בָּאֲבָנִים
וָמֵתָה כִּי עָשְׂתָה נְבָלָה בְּיִשְׂרָאֵל לִזְנוֹת בֵּית אָבִיהָ וּבִעַרְתָּ הָרָע מִקִּרְבֶּךָ:

If a man takes a wife, is intimate with her and despises her.

And he makes libelous charges against her and gives her a bad name, saying, "I took this woman, and when I came to her, I did not find evidence of virginity for her.". . .

If this matter was true, no evidence of the girl's virginity was found.

They shall take the girl out to the entrance of her father's house, and the men of her city shall pelt her with stones, and she shall die, for she did a disgraceful thing in Israel, to commit adultery [in] her father's house, so shall you clear away the evil among you.

TEXT 3

Maimonides, Mishneh Torah, Hilchot Ishut 1:1–2

Rabbi Moshe ben Maimon
(Maimonides, Rambam)
1135–1204

Halachist, philosopher, author, and physician. Maimonides was born in Córdoba, Spain. After the conquest of Córdoba by the Almohads, he fled Spain and eventually settled in Cairo, Egypt. There, he became the leader of the Jewish community and served as court physician to the vizier of Egypt. He is most noted for authoring the *Mishneh Torah*, an encyclopedic arrangement of Jewish law, and for his philosophical work, *Guide for the Perplexed*. His rulings on Jewish law are integral to the formation of halachic consensus.

קודם מתן תורה היה אדם פוגע אשה בשוק אם רצה הוא והיא לישא אותה מכניסה לתוך ביתו ובועלה בינו לבין עצמו ותהיה לו לאשה.

כיון שנתנה תורה נצטוו ישראל שאם ירצה האיש לישא אשה יקנה אותה תחלה בפני עדים ואחר כך תהיה לו לאשה שנאמר כי יקח איש אשה ובא אליה.

וליקוחין אלו מצות עשה של תורה הם. ובאחד משלשה דברים אלו האשה נקנית: בכסף. או בשטר. או בביאה. בביאה ובשטר מהתורה. ובכסף מדברי סופרים.

Before the Torah was given, when a man would meet a woman in the marketplace and he and she decided to marry, he would bring her home, conduct relations in private and thus make her his wife.

Once the Torah was given, the Jews were commanded that when a man desires to marry a woman, he must acquire her as a wife in the presence of witnesses. [Only] after this does she become his wife. This is [alluded to in the verse,] "When a man takes a wife and has relations with her. . . ."

This process of acquisition fulfills [one of] the Torah's positive commandments. The process of acquiring a wife is formalized in three ways: through [the transfer of] money, through [the transfer of a] formal document, and through sexual relations.

Put Your Money Where
Your Mouth Is

TEXT 4

Ibid.

> הארוסה אסורה לבעלה מדברי סופרים כל זמן שהיא בבית אביה.
> והבא על ארוסתו בבית חמיו מכין אותו מכת מרדות. ואפילו אם
> קידשה בביאה אסור לו לבוא עליה ביאה שנייה בבית אביה עד
> שיביא אותה לתוך ביתו ויתיחד עמה ויפרישנה לו. וייחוד זה הוא
> הנקרא כניסה לחופה והוא הנקרא נישואין בכל מקום. והבא על
> ארוסתו לשם נישואין אחר שקידשה משיערה בה קנאה ונעשית
> נשואה והרי היא אשתו לכל דבר:
> כיון שנכנסה הארוסה לחופה הרי זו מותרת לבא עליה בכל עת
> שירצה והרי היא אשתו גמורה לכל דבר.

According to rabbinic law, a consecrated woman is forbidden to engage in sexual relations with her husband as long as she lives in her father's home. A man who has relations with his arusah *in his father-in-law's home is punished with rabbinically-sanctioned lashes.*

Even when [the husband] consecrated [his wife] by having sexual relations with her, he is forbidden to engage in sexual relations with her again until he brings her to his home, enters into privacy with her, and thus sets her aside as his.

This "setting aside" is referred to as entry into the chuppah, and it is universally referred to as "marriage."...

Once a consecrated woman has entered the chuppah, her husband is allowed to have relations with her at any time he desires, and she is considered to be his wife with regard to all matters.

Peulah Nimsheches

A Lecture in Hello

TEXT 5

Maimonides, Mishneh Torah, Hilchot Brachot 11:5–6

העושה מצוה ולא בירך אם מצוה שעדיין עשייתה קיימת מברך
אחר עשייה ואם דבר שעבר הוא אינו מברך.
כיצד הרי שנתעטף בציצית או שלבש תפילין או שישב בסוכה ולא
בירך תחלה חוזר ומברך אחר שנתעטף אשר קדשנו במצותיו וצונו
להתעטף בציצית וכן מברך אחר שלבש להניח תפילין ואחר שישב
לישב בסוכה וכן כל כיוצא באלו.
אבל אם שחט בלא ברכה אינו חוזר אחר שחיטה ומברך אשר
קדשנו במצותיו וצונו על השחיטה וכן אם כסה הדם בלא ברכה או
הפריש תרומה ומעשרות או שטבל ולא בירך אינו חוזר ומברך אחר
עשייה וכן כל כיוצא בזה.

A person who performed a mitzvah, but [mistakenly] did not recite a blessing: If the fulfillment of the mitzvah still continues, he may recite the blessing even though he already performed it. If the mitzvah is a deed that is completed, he should not recite a blessing.

What is implied? When a person wrapped himself in tzitzit, donned tefilin, or sat in a sukkah without reciting a blessing at the outset, after wrapping himself [in tzitzit], he should recite the blessing "Who commanded us to wrap ourselves in tzitzit"; after donning [tefilin], he should recite the blessing, "Who commanded us to put on tefilin"; after sitting [in the sukkah], he should recite the blessing, "Who commanded us to sit in the sukkah." The same applies in all similar situations.

In contrast, if a person slaughtered [an animal] without reciting a blessing, he should not recite the blessing, ". . . who sanctified us with Your commandments and commanded us concerning slaughter," after the slaughter [is completed]. Similarly, if he covered [a fowl's] blood, separated terumah *or the tithes, or immersed himself without reciting a blessing beforehand, he should not recite a blessing afterwards. The same applies in all similar situations.*

TEXT 6

Maimonides, Mishneh Torah, Hilchot Ishut 10:6

וְאִם עָבַר וְנָשָׂא וּבֵירַךְ אֵינוֹ חוֹזֵר וּמְבָרֵךְ.

The wedding blessings may be recited even after several days have passed.

TEXT 7

Rabbi Yosef Rosen, Tzafnat Pane'ach to Mishneh Torah Hilchot Ishut 24:22

אַךְ רַבֵּינוּ הָרַמְבַּ"ם ז"ל סְבִירָא לֵיהּ לְפִי מַה שֶׁכָּתוּב בְּכַמָּה מְקוֹמוֹת דְּנִשּׂוּאִין בְּכָל יוֹם וָיוֹם הֲוָה קִנְיָן חָדָשׁ, לֹא מַהֲנֵי מַה שֶׁכְּבָר נָשָׂאָה.

According to the approach I have proposed in a number of places, Maimonides is of the opinion that marriage is renewed every day. It is not enough that one acquired a legal married status in the past.

Rabbi Yosef Rosen
(Rogatchover Ga'on)
1858–1936
One of the prominent Talmudic scholars of the early 20th century. Born in Rogachev, Belarus, to a Chasidic family, his unusual capabilities were recognized at a young age. At 13 he was brought to Slutzk to study with Rabbi Yosef Ber Soloveitchik. He remained there for a full year, studying primarily with the rabbi's son, the legendary Chaim Soloveitchik. Later, he moved on to Shklov, where he studied with Rabbi Moshe Yehoshua Leib Diskin. After a period in Warsaw, the home city of his wife, he assumed the rabbinate of the Chasidic community in Dvinsk, Latvia. His works, titled *Tzafnat Pane'ach*, are famed for both their depth and difficulty.

Kabbalistic Apocalypse

TEXT 8

Rabbi Shneur Zalman of Liadi, Tanya, Shaar Hayichud Veha'emunah, ch. 1–2

Rabbi Shne'ur Zalman of Liadi
(Alter Rebbe)
1745–1812

Chasidic rebbe, halachic authority, and founder of the Chabad movement. The Alter Rebbe was born in Liozna, Belarus, and was among the principal students of the Magid of Mezeritch. His numerous works include the *Tanya*, an early classic containing the fundamentals of Chabad Chasidism, and *Shulchan Aruch HaRav*, an expanded and reworked code of Jewish law.

הנה כתיב לעולם ה' דברך נצב בשמים. ופי' הבעש"ט ז"ל כי דברך שאמרת יהי רקיע בתוך המים וגו' תיבות ואותיות אלו הן נצבות ועומדות לעולם בתוך רקיע השמים ומלובשות בתוך כל הרקיעים לעולם להחיותם . . .

כי אילו היו האותיות מסתלקות כרגע ח"ו וחוזרות למקורן היו כל השמים אין ואפס ממש והיו כלא היו כלל וכמו קודם מאמר יהי רקיע כו' ממש.

וכן בכל הברואים שבכל העולמות עליונים ותחתונים ואפי' ארץ הלזו הגשמית ובחינת דומם ממש אילו היו מסתלקות ממנה כרגע ח"ו האותיות מעשרה מאמרות שבהן נבראת הארץ בששת ימי בראשית היתה חוזרת לאין ואפס ממש כמו לפני ששת ימי בראשית ממש . . .

והנה מכאן תשובת המינים וגילוי שורש טעותם הכופרים בהשגחה פרטית ובאותות ומופתי התורה שטועים בדמיונם הכוזב שמדמין מעשה ה' עושה שמים וארץ למעשה אנוש ותחבולותיו.

כי כאשר יצא לצורף כלי שוב אין הכלי צריך לידי הצורף כי אף שידיו מסולקות הימנו והולך לו בשוק הכלי קיים בתבניתו וצלמו ממש כאשר יצא מידי הצורף כך מדמין הסכלים האלו מעשה שמים וארץ.

אך טח מראות עיניהם ההבדל הגדול שבין מעשה אנוש ותחבולותיו שהוא יש מיש רק שמשנה הצורה והתמונה מתמונת חתיכת כסף לתמונת כלי למעשה שמים וארץ שהוא יש מאין.

Scripture states: "Forever, oh G-d, Your word stands in the heavens."

The Baal Shemtov, of blessed memory, explained that the words G-d uttered when creating the world, "Let there be an expanse in the midst of the waters," etc., these words and letters forever stand firmly in the heavens, and are forever integrated within the heavens to give them life . . .

If the letters would be withdrawn, if even for a moment, G-d forbid, and returned to their source, all of the heavens would turn to literally nothing, as if they never at all existed, exactly as they were before G-d uttered, "Let there be an expanse," etc.

So it is with all creations, in all the worlds, high and low, even this physical world, the completely inanimate: if the letters of the "ten utterances" from which it was created in six days would be withdrawn for even a moment, G-d forbid, it would return to literally nothing, exactly as before creation . . .

We can now draw an answer to the heretics and expose the root of their mistake, namely those who reject divine providence and the signs and miracles recorded in the Torah. In their false analysis, they compare the work of G-d, creator of heaven and earth, to the work of man and his schemes.

When a craftsman produces a vessel, the vessel no longer needs the craftsman, for even when he is detached from it and leaves to the market, the vessel maintains the exact form it had when shaped by the craftsman. And these fools use this as an analogy for the act of creating heaven and earth.

But their eyes are covered, they do not see the great difference between the work and schemes of man, who creates something from something, and only changes the shape and image, form the image of a piece of metal to the image of a vessel, to the creation of heaven and earth, which is something from nothing.

Desperate Times Call For Desperate Measures

Text 9

The Lubavitcher Rebbe, Likutei Sichot, vol. 5, pp. 177–178

וגם בדיני התורה כן הוא. וכמו בהקדש, אשר "כיון שקיימא לן יש שאלה להקדש הוי כמו בכל רגע ורגע הקדש חדש", כי קדושה ענינה הבדלה והפרשה, ובמילא, חיבורה עם הגשם הוא חיבור ב' הפכים.

וכן בנשואין, שלכמה שיטות "בכל יום ויום הוה קנין חדש"—לפי שיחוד דכר ונוקבא הוא חיבור ב' הפכים.

Rabbi Menachem Mendel Schneerson
1902–1994
The towering Jewish leader of the 20th century, known as "the Lubavitcher Rebbe," or simply as "the Rebbe." Born in southern Ukraine, the Rebbe escaped Nazi-occupied Europe, arriving in the U.S. in June 1941. The Rebbe inspired and guided the revival of traditional Judaism after the European devastation, impacting virtually every Jewish community the world over. The Rebbe often emphasized that the performance of just one additional good deed could usher in the era of Mashiach. The Rebbe's scholarly talks and writings have been printed in more than 200 volumes.

The same is true in halachah. Hekdesh, for example, in the Rogatchover's reasoning, "Inasmuch as the original hekdesh can be revoked, the original pledge is essentially being constantly renewed." This is because by definition, "sanctity" is distant from material matter, so to deem physical property as "sacred" is a fusion of opposites.

So it is with marriage. According to multiple opinions, it is halachically considered as if "every day there is a new act of marriage." This is because the union of male and female is a merger of opposites.

Sustaining the Unsustainable

The Kabbalah of Nagging

TEXT 11

Shemot (Exodus) 34:6–7

וַיַּעֲבֹר ה' עַל פָּנָיו וַיִּקְרָא ה' ה' אֵל רַחוּם וְחַנּוּן אֶרֶךְ אַפַּיִם וְרַב חֶסֶד וֶאֱמֶת:
נֹצֵר חֶסֶד לָאֲלָפִים נֹשֵׂא עָוֹן וָפֶשַׁע וְחַטָּאָה וְנַקֵּה לֹא יְנַקֶּה פֹּקֵד עֲוֹן אָבוֹת עַל בָּנִים וְעַל בְּנֵי בָנִים עַל שִׁלֵשִׁים וְעַל רִבֵּעִים:

Lord, Lord, benevolent G-d, Who is compassionate and gracious, slow to anger and abundant in loving kindness and truth, preserving kindness for thousands, forgiving iniquity and rebellion and sin; yet, He does not completely clear [of sin], He visits the iniquity of parents on children and children's children, to the third and fourth generations.

Lucky Thirteen

TEXT 12A

Rabbi Yitzchak Luria, The Arizal, Eitz Chaim Sha'ar 13:9

הם על זה הסדר: א-ל א', רחום ב', וחנון ג', ארך ד', אפים ה', לפי
שארך אפים מורה על ב' מדות יחד ולזה לא אמר ארך אף אלא
אפים, ורב חסד ו', ואמת ז', נוצר חסד ח', לאלפים ט', נושא עון י',
ופשע י"א, וחטאה י"ב, ונקה י"ג.

They are in this order: 1. Lord; 2. benevolent; 3. compassionate; 4. slow; 5. to anger—"slow to anger" includes two attributes of mercy which is why it is written in plural; 6. abundant in kindness; 7. and truth; 8. preserving kindness; 9. for thousands; 10. forgiving iniquity; 11. and rebellion; 12. and sin; and 13. clear [of sin].

Rabbi Yitzchak Luria
1534–1572
Known by the acronym "Arizal," or simply "the Ari." Founder of the Lurianic school of kabbalah. Born in Jerusalem; raised in Egypt; died in Safed. Rabbi Luria studied Talmud under Rabbi Betzalel Ashkenazi, compiler of the *Shitah Mekubetzet*. Despite his youth, he was accepted among the rabbinic elite of Safed. The Ari never recorded his teachings; they were collected and transcribed by his disciples. His leading disciple, Rabbi Chaim Vital, is generally considered the most authoritative recorder of the Arizal's teachings.

Men are From Notzar, Woman Are From Nakkeh

TEXT 12B

Ibid. Sha'ar Haklalim 5; 13:9

והנה אלו ב' תיקונים נקרא מזלא, והם ב' מזלות, ופי' מזלא מלשון
תזל כטל אמרתי, שהוא משך השערות באורך מלמעלה למטה, ואין
בכל הי"ג תיקונים האלו שיהיה נקרא כך אלא אלו השנים, העליון
נקרא 'נוצר' תיקון הח', והתחתון נקרא 'ונקה' תיקון י"ג, ושניהן כל
אחד נקרא מזלא . . י"ג ונקה הוא המזל הב' ונקרא תיקון י"ג.
ואמנם ב' מזלות האלו שוכבים זה על זה והם דכורא ונוקבא, ואבא
יונק מן הח' ואמא יונקת מן הי"ג הרי ביארנו י"ג תיקוני דיקנא

Know that in the beard of "the long face" there are two mazalot, *the upper* mazal *is "preserving kindness"— the eighth attribute, and the lower* mazal *is "clear [of sin]"—the thirteenth attribute . . .*

. . . These two attributes are called mazal. *They are two* mazalot. *The meaning of the word* mazal *is from the root word of the biblical "my lesson will drip (tizal) like rain," it is the extension of the beard lengthwise from above to below. None of the other attributes are called* mazal *aside for these two. The upper [of them] is called* notzar—*the eighth attribute, and the lower one is called* nake—*the thirteenth attribute. Both of them, they are each called* mazal.

Indeed, these two mazalot *lie on one another, they are male and female. The "father" draws sustenance from the eighth attribute, and the "mother" draws sustenance from the thirteenth. We have now explained the Thirteen Attributes of Kindness.*

TEXT 13

The Lubavitcher Rebbe, Likutei Sichot, *vol. 20, p. 576*

די חתונה זאל זיין בשעה טובה ומוצלחת, ובמזל טוב מזל טוב, כנוסח הרגיל בשייכות לחתונה כנגד ב' מזלות דנוצר ונקה, ובנישואין ב' המזלות דחתן וכלה מתאחדין.

May the wedding be in a good and auspicious hour, and with mazel tov, mazel tov, as is the regular phrase used in the context of marriage. This corresponds to the two mazals notzar *and* nake. *In a marriage, the* mazals *merge.*

Likutei Sichot
Widely considered the Rebbe's magnum opus, the 39 volumes of Likutei Sichot feature scholarly essays relating to themes in the weekly Torah portions and the Jewish holidays. The Rebbe initially conveyed these concepts in his public talks and subsequently reworked them for publication. In some volumes, the essays appear in Yiddish, while in others they are in Hebrew. Most volumes also present a collection of the Rebbe's correspondence.

9

KI TAVO

Mind over Matter

The Tefilin *Mind Game*

*Dedicated by the **Serzon** Family in honor of **Rabbi Eli** and **Rivky Shifrin**, dear family friends and spiritual leaders. May they and the extended Shifrin and Halberstam families be blessed with good health, happiness, nachas, and success in their personal and communal endeavors. May you go from strength to strength!*

PARSHAH OVERVIEW
Ki Tavo

Moses instructs the people of Israel: When you enter the land that G-d is giving to you as your eternal heritage, and you settle it and cultivate it, bring the first-ripened fruits (bikkurim) of your orchard to the Holy Temple, and declare your gratitude for all that G-d has done for you.

Our parshah also includes the laws of the tithes given to the Levites and to the poor, and detailed instructions on how to proclaim the blessings and the curses on Mount Gerizim and Mount Ebal—as discussed in the beginning of the parshah of Re'eh. Moses reminds the people that they are G-d's chosen people, and that they, in turn, have chosen G-d.

The latter part of Ki Tavo consists of the tochachah ("rebuke"). After listing the blessings with which G-d will reward the people when they follow the laws of the Torah, Moses gives a long, harsh account of the bad things—illness, famine, poverty, and exile—that shall befall them if they abandon G-d's commandments.

Moses concludes by telling the people that only today, forty years after their birth as a people, have they attained "a heart to know, eyes to see, and ears to hear."

Secure the Border

Farewell Address

TEXT 1

Devarim (Deuteronomy) 28:1–10

וְהָיָה אִם שָׁמוֹעַ תִּשְׁמַע בְּקוֹל יְקֹוָק אֱלֹהֶיךָ לִשְׁמֹר לַעֲשׂוֹת אֶת כָּל
מִצְוֹתָיו אֲשֶׁר אָנֹכִי מְצַוְּךָ הַיּוֹם וּנְתָנְךָ ה' אֱלֹקֶיךָ עֶלְיוֹן עַל כָּל גּוֹיֵי הָאָרֶץ:
וּבָאוּ עָלֶיךָ כָּל הַבְּרָכוֹת הָאֵלֶּה וְהִשִּׂיגֻךָ כִּי תִשְׁמַע בְּקוֹל ה' אֱלֹקֶיךָ:
בָּרוּךְ אַתָּה בָּעִיר וּבָרוּךְ אַתָּה בַּשָּׂדֶה:
בָּרוּךְ פְּרִי בִטְנְךָ וּפְרִי אַדְמָתְךָ וּפְרִי בְהֶמְתֶּךָ שְׁגַר אֲלָפֶיךָ
וְעַשְׁתְּרוֹת צֹאנֶךָ:
בָּרוּךְ טַנְאֲךָ וּמִשְׁאַרְתֶּךָ:
בָּרוּךְ אַתָּה בְּבֹאֶךָ וּבָרוּךְ אַתָּה בְּצֵאתֶךָ:
יִתֵּן ה' אֶת אֹיְבֶיךָ הַקָּמִים עָלֶיךָ נִגָּפִים לְפָנֶיךָ בְּדֶרֶךְ אֶחָד יֵצְאוּ אֵלֶיךָ
וּבְשִׁבְעָה דְרָכִים יָנוּסוּ לְפָנֶיךָ:
יְצַו ה' אִתְּךָ אֶת הַבְּרָכָה בַּאֲסָמֶיךָ וּבְכֹל מִשְׁלַח יָדֶךָ וּבֵרַכְךָ בָּאָרֶץ אֲשֶׁר
ה' אֱלֹקֶיךָ נֹתֵן לָךְ:
יְקִימְךָ ה' לוֹ לְעַם קָדוֹשׁ כַּאֲשֶׁר נִשְׁבַּע לָךְ כִּי תִשְׁמֹר אֶת מִצְוֹת ה'
אֱלֹקֶיךָ וְהָלַכְתָּ בִּדְרָכָיו:
וְרָאוּ כָּל עַמֵּי הָאָרֶץ כִּי שֵׁם ה' נִקְרָא עָלֶיךָ וְיָרְאוּ מִמֶּךָּ:

And it will be if you obey the Lord, your G-d, to observe to fulfill all His commandments which I command you this day, the Lord, your G-d, will place you supreme above all the nations of the earth.

And all these blessings will come upon you and cleave to you, if you obey the Lord, your G-d.

You shall be blessed in the city, and you shall be blessed in the field.

Blessed will be the fruit of your womb, the fruit of your soil, the fruit of your livestock, the offspring of your cattle, and the flocks of your sheep.

Blessed will be your basket and your kneading bowl.

You shall be blessed when you come, and you shall be blessed when you depart.

G-d will cause your enemies who rise up against you to be beaten before you; they will come out against you in one direction, but they will flee from you in seven directions.

G-d will order the blessing to be with you in your granaries, and in every one of your endeavors, and He will bless you in the land which the Lord, your G-d, is giving you.

G-d will establish you as His holy people as He swore to you, if you observe the commandments of the Lord, your G-d, and walk in His ways.

Then all the peoples of the earth will see that the name of G-d is called upon you, and they will fear you.

A New Approach to Security

TEXT 2

Talmud Tractate Berachot 6a

Babylonian Talmud

A literary work of monumental proportions that draws upon the legal, spiritual, intellectual, ethical, and historical traditions of Judaism. The 37 tractates of the Babylonian Talmud contain the teachings of the Jewish sages from the period after the destruction of the Second Temple through the fifth century CE. It has served as the primary vehicle for the transmission of the Oral Law and the education of Jews over the centuries; it is the entry point for all subsequent legal, ethical, and theological Jewish scholarship.

מנין שהתפילין עוז הם לישראל דכתיב "וראו כל עמי הארץ כי שם ה' נקרא עליך ויראו ממך", ותניא רבי אליעזר הגדול אומר אלו תפילין שבראש.

From where do we know that tefilin *give Jews strength? Scripture states, "And all the nations of the earth will see that G-d's name is upon you, and they shall fear you." It was stated in a* Beraita: *Rabbi Eliezer "the great one" said, "This refers to the head* tefilin."

TEXT 3

Tosafot, ad loc.

Tosafot

A collection of French and German Talmudic commentaries written during the 12th and 13th centuries. Among the most famous authors of *Tosafot* are Rabbi Yaakov Tam, Rabbi Shimshon ben Avraham of Sens, and Rabbi Yitschak ("the Ri"). Printed in almost all editions of the Talmud, these commentaries are fundamental to basic Talmudic study.

לפי שהן בגבהו של ראש ונראין דשייך בהו "וראו", אבל תפילין של יד מכוסין דכתיב 'לך לאות על ידך' ולא לאחרים לאות.

Because head tefilin *are worn high on the head, the verse, "and [the nations] will see," applies to them. The hand* tefilin, *by contrast, are generally concealed, congruent with the verse which states, "A sign for you," and not a sign for others.*

Double Points

613

TEXT 4A

Devarim (Deuteronomy) 33:4

תּוֹרָה צִוָּה לָנוּ מֹשֶׁה מוֹרָשָׁה קְהִלַּת יַעֲקֹב:

The Torah that Moses commanded us is a legacy for the congregation of Jacob.

TEXT 4B

Talmud Tractate Makot 23b-24a

דרש רבי שמלאי: שש מאות ושלש עשרה מצות נאמרו לו למשה; שלש מאות וששים וחמש לאוין כמנין ימות החמה, ומאתים וארבעים ושמונה עשה כנגד איבריו של אדם. אמר רב המנונא: מאי קרא? תורה צוה לנו משה מורשה; תורה בגימטריא שית מאה וחד סרי הוי אנכי ולא יהיה לך מפי הגבורה שמענום.

Rav Simlai taught: Moses was taught by G-d 613 mitzvos. 365 negative mitzvos, corresponding to the solar year, and 248 positive mitzvos, corresponding to man's limbs.

Rav Hamnuna says: What is the Scriptural source for this idea? The verse states, "The Torah that Moses commanded us is a legacy." [The Hebrew word] "Torah" has the numeric value of 611. "Anochi" and "Lo Yihiye Lecha" [the first two of the Ten Commandments], we heard from directly G-d.

TEXT 5

Maimonides, Sefer Hamitzvot, Rule 11

אין ראוי למנות חלקי המצוה בפרט חלק חלק בפני עצמו כשיהיה המקובץ מהם מצוה אחת: פעמים יהיה הצווי האחד שהוא מצוה אחת יש לו חלקים רבים. כמו מצות לולב שהיא ארבעה מינים. הנה לא נאמר כי פרי עץ הדר מצוה בפני עצמה וכפות תמרים מצוה בפני עצמה וענף עץ עבות מצוה בפני עצמה וערבי נחל מצוה בפני עצמה. לפי שאלו כלם הם חלקי המצוה. כי הוא צוה לקבצם ואחר קבוצם תהיה המצוה לקיחת הכל ביד ביום הידוע.

When there are multiple elements of a mitzvah that converge into a single mitzvah, one ought not to count them as separate mitzvot. It is possible that a single commandment will comprise multiple elements. Take the mitzvah of lulav, for example—it is four distinct species. It would not make sense to say that "a beautiful fruit" is one mitzvah, "date palms" another, "a braided branch" another, and "willows of the stream" another—for they all are part of one, single mitzvah:

Rabbi Moshe ben Maimon

(Maimonides, Rambam)
1135–1204

Halachist, philosopher, author, and physician. Maimonides was born in Córdoba, Spain. After the conquest of Córdoba by the Almohads, he fled Spain and eventually settled in Cairo, Egypt. There, he became the leader of the Jewish community and served as court physician to the vizier of Egypt. He is most noted for authoring the *Mishneh Torah*, an encyclopedic arrangement of Jewish law, and for his philosophical work, *Guide for the Perplexed*. His rulings on Jewish law are integral to the formation of halachic consensus.

G-d commanded us to gather these items together and thereafter perform a mitzvah by collectively taking them in hand on the appropriate day.

TEXT 6

Maimonides, Mishneh Torah, Hilchot Tefilin 4:4

תפלה של ראש אינה מעכבת של יד ושל יד אינה מעכבת של ראש מפני שהן שתי מצות זו לעצמה וזו לעצמה.

The [absence of] head tefilin *does not preclude [wearing* tefilin*] on the arm, and similarly, the [absence of] arm* tefilin *does not preclude [wearing* tefilin*] on the head. They are two independent* mitzvot.

To Be or To Do

TEXT 7

Rabbi Yosef Rosen, The Rogatchover Ga'on,
Tzafnat Pane'ach, Hilchot Tefilin 4:4

Rabbi Yosef Rosen
(Rogatchover Ga'on)
1858–1936

One of the prominent talmudic
scholars of the early 20th
century. Born in Rogachev,
Belarus, to a Chasidic family,
his unusual capabilities were
recognized at a young age.
At 13 he was brought to
Slutzk to study with Rabbi
Yosef Ber Soloveitchik. He
remained there for a full year,
studying primarily with the
rabbi's son, the legendary
Chaim Soloveitchik. Later, he
moved on to Shklov, where
he studied with Rabbi Moshe
Yehoshua Leib Diskin. After
a period in Warsaw, the home
city of his wife, he assumed
the rabbinate of the Chasidic
community in Dvinsk, Latvia.
His works, titled *Tzafnat
Pane'ach*, are famed for both
their depth and difficulty.

והנה באמת כך, דגבי תפילין של יד המצווה היא ההנחה או הקשירה,
אבל תפילין של ראש המצווה שיהיה מונח.

The truth is, the mitzvah of hand tefilin *is the act of
donning or tying. With regards the head* tefilin, *however, the mitzvah is that they be worn.*

TEXT 8A

Devarim (Deuteronomy) 6:8

וּקְשַׁרְתָּם לְאוֹת עַל יָדֶךָ וְהָיוּ לְטֹטָפֹת בֵּין עֵינֶיךָ:

*Bind them as a sign on your hand and they will be a
symbol on your forehead.*

TEXT 8B

The Lubavitcher Rebbe, Likutei Sichot, vol. 39, p. 24

Rabbi Menachem Mendel Schneerson
1902–1994

יסודו בלשון הכתוב עצמו, "וקשרתם לאות על ידיך והיו לטוטופות בין עיניך", דגבי של יד נקט הכתוב מעשה הקשירה, ואילו בתפילין של ראש נאמר "והיו".

The towering Jewish leader of the 20th century, known as "the Lubavitcher Rebbe," or simply as "the Rebbe." Born in southern Ukraine, the Rebbe escaped Nazi-occupied Europe, arriving in the U.S. in June 1941. The Rebbe inspired and guided the revival of traditional Judaism after the European devastation, impacting virtually every Jewish community the world over. The Rebbe often emphasized that the performance of just one additional good deed could usher in the era of Mashiach. The Rebbe's scholarly talks and writings have been printed in more than 200 volumes.

The Rogatchover draws his conclusion from the verse, "Bind them as a sign on your hand and they will be a symbol on your forehead." Regarding hand tefilin, *Scripture references the act of tying, whereas regarding the head* tefilin, *Scripture only states, "they shall be."*

Knowledge is Power

A Wiring System

TEXT 9

Shulchan Aruch Admur Hazaken, Hilchot Tefilin 25:11

Rabbi Shneur Zalman of Liadi
(Alter Rebbe)
1745–1812
Chasidic rebbe, halachic authority, and founder of the Chabad movement. The Alter Rebbe was born in Liozna, Belarus, and was among the principal students of the Magid of Mezeritch. His numerous works include the *Tanya*, an early classic containing the fundamentals of Chabad Chasidism, and *Shulchan Aruch HaRav*, an expanded and reworked code of Jewish law.

יכוין בהנחת התפילין שצוונו הקדוש ברוך הוא לכתוב ד' פרשיות אלו שיש בהם יחוד שמו ויציאת מצרים ולהניחן על הזרוע כנגד הלב ועל הראש כנגד המוח כדי שנזכור נסים ונפלאות שעשה עמנו שהם מורים על יחודו ואשר לו הכח והממשלה לעשות בעליונים ובתחתונים כרצונו וישעבד להקדוש ברוך הוא הנשמה שהיא במוח וגם תאות ומחשבות לבו לעבודתו יתברך ועל ידי הנחת תפילין יזכור את הבורא יתברך וימעיט הנאותיו.

When putting on tefilin, *one should have in mind that G-d commanded us to write these four biblical excerpts that contain His unity and the Exodus from Egypt, and to place them on the arm opposite the heart and the head opposite the mind. He so commanded us so that we remember the miracles and wonders he did for us that attest to His unity, and that He has the power and ability to do as He wants in the upper and lower worlds. The goal is to subjugate the soul which is in the mind and the heart's desires to divine service. Thus, through putting on* tefilin *he will recall the Creator and decrease his primal desires.*

TEXT 10

Tanya ch. 17

ובזה יובן מה שכתוב "כי קרוב אליך הדבר מאד בפיך ובלבבך
לעשותו", דלכאורה הוא בלבבך נגד החוש שלנו [והתורה היא
נצחית] שאין קרוב מאד הדבר להפך לבו מתאוות עולם הזה לאהבת
ה' באמת וכמו שכתוב בגמרא "אטו יראה מילתא זוטרתי היא?!"
וכל שכן אהבה! וגם אמרו רז"ל דצדיקים דוקא לבם ברשותם.
אלא דלעשותו רוצה לומר האהבה המביאה לידי עשיית המצות
בלבד. ודבר זה קרוב מאד ונקל לכל אדם אשר יש לו מוח בקדקדו
כי מוחו ברשותו ויכול להתבונן בו ככל אשר יחפוץ וכשיתבונן בו
בגדולת אין סוף ברוך הוא ממילא יוליד במוחו על כל פנים האהבה
לה' לדבקה בו בקיום מצותיו ותורתו . . . והמוח שליט בטבעו
ותולדתו על חלל השמאלי שבלב ועל פיו ועל כל האברים שהם
כלי המעשה.

*This explains the verse, "For it is very close to you to
do, in your mouth and in your heart." This seemingly
contradicts common experience [and Torah is eternal].
It is not "close" to steer the heart from the world's
pleasures to true love of G-d. As the Talmud states,
"Do you think fear [of G-d] is a small matter?!"—and
all the more so love [of G-d]. Also our Sages said that
only the righteous control their emotions.*

Rather, when it states "to do," Scripture speaks only of the love that promotes practical performance of mitzvot *alone. . . .*

This is very close and easy for any intelligent person, as he controls his mind, and can use it to contemplate anything he desires. When he contemplates G-d's infinite greatness, he will automatically produce love of G-d at least in his mind, motivating him to cleave to G-d by fulfilling Torah and mitzvot.

The mind naturally rules the heart's "left chamber" and the mouth and all the acting limbs.

TEXT 11

The Lubavitcher Rebbe, Likutei Sichot, vol. 39, p. 28

ועל פי זה יש לבאר החילוק הנזכר לעיל בין תפילין של יד ותפילין
של ראש (דתפילין של יד מצותן רק מעשה הקשירה, ואילו תפילין
של ראש היא מצוה תמידית, "שיהיה מונח") – בפנימיות הענינים:
בנוגע למדות שבלב, הרי אין לבו של אדם (בינוני – שהיא מדת
כל אדם) ברשותו "להפך לבו מתאוות עולם הזה לאהבת ה'
באמת" (דצדיקים דוקא לבם ברשותם), ולכן אין מצות תפילין
של יד – דהיינו שעבוד תאוות הלב – "שיהיה מונח", כי אם רק
מעשה הקשירה.

זאת אומרת, דאף על פי שאין האדם יכול להפוך את לבו מתאוות
לבו לאהבת ה' באמת, שיהיה משועבד בתמידיות לאהבת ה', מכל
מקום עליו לקשור את לבו, בדרך אתכפיא, לשלוט על עצמו שלא
להוציא תאוותו מן הכח אל הפועל.

מה שאין כן בנוגע למוחו, הרי "מוחו ברשותו" של כל אחד ואחד
מישראל, ש"יכול להתבונן בו בכל אשר יחפוץ", ולכן מצות תפילין
של ראש היא "שיהיה מונח", היינו שיהיה משועבד באופן תמידי
לעבודתו יתברך.

We can now explain the difference between the mitzvah of the hand tefilin vs. the head tefilin discussed above, namely that with the former, the mitzvah is the act of tying, whereas with the latter, the mitzvah is a constant mitzvah—that they be on your head.

When it comes to emotions, the reality is that the average person cannot fundamentally change their heart from primal desires to G-dly ones. Such mastery is the domain of the righteous. As such, the mitzvah of the hand tefilin—namely, disciplining the heart—is not that they "be worn," rather the act of tying.

Namely: Though a person cannot transform his or her heart from material desire to true love of G-d in a way that the heart is constantly infatuated with G-d, it is still incumbent upon the person to tie his or her heart, forcefully so, to control themselves so as not to actually carry out their material desires.

By contrast, when speaking of the mind, a person does have control over their mind, for he or she can always ponder whatever they wish. As such, the mitzvah of the hand tefilin is that they "be worn," namely that the mind be consistently regulated to G-d.

10

ROSH HASHANAH

The Need to Be Needy

Complacency Is the Graveyard of Growth

*Dedicated to **Mark** and **Rebecca Bolinsky** in appreciation of their partnership
in bringing the light of Torah to communities around the globe.*

OVERVIEW
Rosh Hashanah

The festival of Rosh Hashanah—the name means "Head of the Year"—is observed for two days beginning on 1 Tishrei, the first day of the Jewish year. It is the anniversary of the creation of Adam and Eve, the first man and woman, and their first actions toward the realization of mankind's role in G-d's world.

Rosh Hashanah thus emphasizes the special relationship between G-d and humanity: our dependence upon G-d as our creator and sustainer, and G-d's dependence upon us as the ones who make His presence known and felt in His world. Each year on Rosh Hashanah, "all inhabitants of the world pass before G-d like a flock of sheep," and it is decreed in the heavenly court "who shall live, and who shall die . . . who shall be impoverished, and who shall be enriched; who shall fall and who shall rise." But this is also the day we proclaim G-d King of the Universe. The kabbalists teach that the continued existence of the universe is dependent upon the renewal of the Divine desire for a world when we accept G-d's kingship each year on Rosh Hashanah.

The central observance of Rosh Hashanah is the sounding of the shofar, *the ram's horn, which also represents* the trumpet blast of a people's coronation of their king. The cry of the shofar is also a call to repentance, for Rosh Hashanah is also the anniversary of man's first sin and his repentance thereof, and serves as the first of the "Ten Days of Repentance" which culminate in Yom Kippur, the Day of Atonement. Another significance of the shofar is to recall the Binding of Isaac, which also occurred on Rosh Hashanah, in which a ram took Isaac's place as an offering to G-d; we evoke Abraham's readiness to sacrifice his son, and plead that the merit of his deed should stand by us as we pray for a year of life, health, and prosperity. Altogether, we listen to one hundred shofar blasts over the course of the Rosh Hashanah services.

Additional Rosh Hashanah observances include: a) Eating a piece of apple dipped in honey, to symbolize our desire for a sweet year, and other special foods symbolic of the new year's blessings. b) Blessing one another with the words "Leshanah tovah tikateiv veteichateim," "May you be inscribed and sealed for a good year." c) Tashlich, a special prayer said near a body of water (an ocean, river, pond, etc.), in evocation of the verse, "And You shall cast their sins into the depths of the sea." And as with every major Jewish holiday, after candlelighting and prayers we recite Kiddush and make a blessing on the challah.

TEXT 1A

Pre-Rosh-Hashanah Prayer of Supplication

כדלים וכרשים דפקנו דלתיך.
דלתיך דפקנו רחום וחנון, נא אל תשיבינו ריקם מלפניך.
מלפניך מלכינו ריקם אל תשיבינו, כי אתה שומע תפילה.

Humble and impoverished, we knock on Your doors.

We knock on Your doors, Merciful and Gracious One, please do not turn us back empty handed.

From Your presence, our King, turn us not back empty handed, for You are One who listens to prayer.

TEXT 1B

Liturgical Text of the Daily Prayer

מוציא אסירים, פודה ענווים, עוזר דלים.
העונה לעמו ישראל בעת שועם אליו.

G-d frees the captives, redeems the humble, and helps the needy.

He answers His people, Israel, when they cry out to Him.

A Time for Poverty

TEXT 2

Talmud Tractate Beitzah 16a

"תקעו בחדש שופר בכסה ליום חגנו." איזהו חג שהחדש מתכסה
בו? הוי אומר זה ראש השנה.

"Sound the shofar on the New Moon, in concealment, the day of our festival." Which festival falls when the moon is concealed? I would say it is Rosh Hashanah.

Babylonian Talmud

A literary work of monumental proportions that draws upon the legal, spiritual, intellectual, ethical, and historical traditions of Judaism. The 37 tractates of the Babylonian Talmud contain the teachings of the Jewish sages from the period after the destruction of the Second Temple through the fifth century CE. It has served as the primary vehicle for the transmission of the Oral Law and the education of Jews over the centuries; it is the entry point for all subsequent legal, ethical, and theological Jewish scholarship.

TEXT 3A

Tehillim (Psalms) 118:5

מִן הַמֵּצַר קָרָאתִי יָ-הּ עָנָנִי בַמֶּרְחָב יָ-הּ:

From the straits I called G-d; G-d answered me with a vast expanse.

TEXT 3B

Shulchan Aruch Harav, Orach Chaim 190:20

Rabbi Shne'ur Zalman of Liadi (Alter Rebbe) 1745–1812

Chasidic rebbe, halachic authority, and founder of the Chabad movement. The Alter Rebbe was born in Liozna, Belarus, and was among the principal students of the Magid of Mezeritch. His numerous works include the *Tanya*, an early classic containing the fundamentals of Chabad Chasidism, and *Shulchan Aruch HaRav*, an expanded and reworked code of Jewish law.

התוקע בצד הרחב של השופר לא יצא. רמז לדבר, "מן המיצר".

One who blows the shofar from its broad side does not fulfill the obligation. This is implied by the verse, "From the straits I called G-d."

TEXT 4A

Talmud Tractate Rosh Hashanah, 16b

ואמר רבי יצחק כל שנה שרשה בתחלתה מתעשרת בסופה שנאמר, "מראשית השנה," מרשית כתיב, "ועד אחרית," סופה שיש לה אחרית.

Rabbi Yitzchak said: Every year that begins in poverty ends in prosperity as the verse states, "From the beginning of the year until the end of the year." The verse is spelled as if it is written, "From the poverty of the year, until the good ending of the year."

TEXT 4B

Rashi, ad loc.

שישראל עושין עצמן רשין בראש השנה לדבר תחנונים ותפלה
כענין שנאמר, "תחנונים ידבר רש".

Jews humble themselves on Rosh Hashanah to speak
in supplication and in prayer, as in the verse, "A poor
man speaks in supplication."

Dawn Follows Dark

TEXT 5

Bereishit (Genesis) 1:5

וַיִּקְרָא אֱלֹקִים לָאוֹר יוֹם וְלַחֹשֶׁךְ קָרָא לָיְלָה וַיְהִי עֶרֶב וַיְהִי בֹקֶר
יוֹם אֶחָד:

And G-d called the light day, and the darkness He
called night, and it was evening and it was morning,
one day.

TEXT 6

Rabbi Dov Ber of Mezeritch, Ohr Torah, 84B

Rabbi Dov Ber "the Magid" of Mezeritch
d. 1772
Was the primary disciple and eventual successor of the Baal Shem Tov. Amongst his disciples were the founders of various Chasidic dynasties, including Rabbi Nachum of Chernobyl, Rabbi Levi Yitzchak of Berditchev, and Rabbi Shne'ur Zalman of Liadi. His teachings, recorded by his students, appear in various volumes including the *Magid Devarav LeYaakov*.

"וְעֵינֵינוּ מְאִירוֹת כַּשֶּׁמֶשׁ וְכַיָּרֵחַ," הַשֶּׁמֶשׁ אֵינוֹ מְקַבֵּל מִשּׁוּם דָּבָר, וְהַיָּרֵחַ הִיא מְקַבֶּלֶת הָאוֹר מִן הַשֶּׁמֶשׁ?

אַךְ בָּזֶה יֵשׁ לָהּ יוֹתֵר תַּעֲנוּג, כִּי הַשֶּׁמֶשׁ אֵין לָהּ תַּעֲנוּג, כִּי תַּעֲנוּג תְּמִידִי אֵינוֹ תַּעֲנוּג, אֲבָל הַיָּרֵחַ יֵשׁ לָהּ תַּעֲנוּג בְּהַגִּיעַ לָהּ אוֹר. וְהַתַּעֲנוּג הוּא מִדְּרֵיגָה גְּדוֹלָה . . . כְּמָשָׁל עָנִי אֶחָד שֶׁמִּשְׂתַּכֵּר מֵאָה זְהוּבִים יֵשׁ לוֹ יוֹתֵר תַּעֲנוּג מֵהַמֶּלֶךְ.

וְהָאָדָם צָרִיךְ לֶאֱחוֹז בִּשְׁנֵיהֶם.

"May our eyes be luminous like the sun and the moon." The sun is the source of its own light, the moon, by contrast, receives its light from the sun. This raises a question, if our eyes are as luminous as the sun, what more is to be gained by being luminous like the moon?

The answer is that the moon takes more delight in luminescence than the sun. The sun does not delight in its luminescence inasmuch as she is constantly luminous and constant delight is not pleasurable. The moon, however, receives light only on occasion and therefore delights when it receives light. . . . This is analogous to a poor man, who takes more delight in earning a hundred gold coins, than the king delights in his vast treasures.

A person must strive for both: the constant luminescence of the sun and the delight taken by the moon.

"Like a Red Trapping on a White Horse"

TEXT 7

Talmud Tractate Chagigah 9B

מאי דכתיב, "הנה צרפתיך, ולא בכסף, בחרתיך בכור עוני?"
מלמד שחזר הקדוש ברוך הוא על כל מדות טובות ליתן לישראל
ולא מצא אלא עניות. אמר שמואל ואיתימא רב יוסף היינו דאמרי
אינשי יאה עניותא ליהודאי כי ברזא סומקא לסוסיא חיורא.

What is the meaning of the verse, "Behold I have refined you but not as silver; I have afflicted you in the furnace of affliction?"

It teaches us that G-d reviewed all the good qualities with an eye toward giving them to the Jewish people, but He found only one: poverty. Shmuel said, and others say it was Rabbi Joseph, who said: This accords with the popular saying, "Poverty befits Israel like a red trapping on a white horse."

Prelude to Dawn

New Growth

TEXT 8

The Lubavitcher Rebbe, Kovetz 11 Nissan, 5762, p. 125

Rabbi Menachem Mendel Schneerson
1902–1994

The towering Jewish leader of the 20th century, known as "the Lubavitcher Rebbe," or simply as "the Rebbe." Born in southern Ukraine, the Rebbe escaped Nazi-occupied Europe, arriving in the U.S. in June 1941. The Rebbe inspired and guided the revival of traditional Judaism after the European devastation, impacting virtually every Jewish community the world over. The Rebbe often emphasized that the performance of just one additional good deed could usher in the era of Mashiach. The Rebbe's scholarly talks and writings have been printed in more than 200 volumes.

כתוב בגמרא בנוגע לרב זירא ש"כי סליק לארעא דישראל יתיב מאה תעניתא דלשתכח גמרא בבלאה מיניה, כי היכא דלא נטרדי," ויוכל ללמוד תלמוד ירושלמי.

שמכיון שרבי זירא רצה להתעלות מדרגא פחותה–דרגת תלמוד בבלי, לדרגא נעלית יותר–דרגת תלמוד ירושלמי, היה צריך להיות אצלו תחילה ענין השכחה בתלמוד בבלי–הדרגא התחתונה, הנפילה ממדריגה הראשונה. ששכחה הוא ענין הנפילה בכדי שיוכל להתעלות אחר זה למדריגה נעלית יותר–דרגת לימוד תלמוד ירושלמי.

אך ענין השכחה והנפילה שהיתה לו בין תלמוד בבלי לתלמוד ירושלמי, אינה נקראת נפילה אלא לגבי מדריגתו הראשונה, ולא לגבי שאר כל אדם חס ושלום.

The Talmud tells us that Rabbi Zeira "fasted for one hundred days when he arrived in Israel in an attempt to forget the Babylonian style of Talmudic study so that it would not interfere" with his transition to the Israeli style of Talmudic study.

Rabbi Zeira wanted to elevate his level of Talmudic study from the inferior Babylonian style to the superior Israeli style. To do so, he had to forget the inferior level so that it shouldn't interfere with the superior level. During that intermediate point, when he had already forgotten the Babylonian style, but had yet to acquire the Israeli style, he was in a fallen state. But the purpose of this fall was to rise to an even higher level, namely the Israeli style of study.

The forgetting and falling that he experienced is only a fall for someone like himself, who was at a lofty level of study before he fasted. However, his level of study even during the fall was greater than that of ordinary students.

Only With G-d

TEXT 9

Rabbi Yosef Yitzchak Schneersohn of Lubavitch,
Sefer Hamaamarim, 5704

Rabbi Yosef Yitzchak Schneersohn
(Rayatz, Frierdiker Rebbe, Previous Rebbe)
1880–1950

Chasidic rebbe, prolific writer, and Jewish activist. Rabbi Yosef Yitzchak, the sixth leader of the Chabad movement, actively promoted Jewish religious practice in Soviet Russia and was arrested for these activities. After his release from prison and exile, he settled in Warsaw, Poland, from where he fled Nazi occupation, and arrived in New York in 1940. Settling in Brooklyn, Rabbi Schneersohn worked to revitalize American Jewish life. His son-in law, Rabbi Menachem Mendel Schneerson, succeeded him as the leader of the Chabad movement.

. . . במדרש רבה איתא: כתיב, "הזורעים בדמעה ברנה יקצורו"
דהקצירה ברנה הוא לפי ערך הזריעה בדמעה.
וכן הוא גם בגשמיות, כמו במשא ומתן בפרנסה, שאי אפשר לאדם
להרויח בעסקיו כי אם אחר היגיעה ופיזור הנפש. שמכניס הון רב
בעסקיו, הן של עצמו, והן של אחרים שלוה על משכנות בתשלום
רוחים גדולים, והכל כאשר לכל מכניס בהעסקים. וכמה פעמים
הרי הוא מסכן את כל הרכוש שלו ושל אחרים בסכנת איבוד הכל
והוא מצטער בצער גדול יסורים גדולים לצלן רחמנא מכמה מניעות
ועכובים עד שיאמר נואש לנפשו ויהיה לבו נשבה... ומקרב

לבו יפנה להשם בתחנונים לחוס ולרחם עליו, ואזי דוקא יצליח לו
השם . . .

וכן הוא ברוחניות כמו בעסק התורה שזהו על ידי יגיעה דוקא . . .
ולפעמים יהיה בצער ויסורים גדולים רחמנא לצלן מהעדר הידיעה,
ומאד לא טוב לו בזה עד שמואס בחייו ממש, ונשבר לבו ורוחו
בקרבו, ואז דוקא יאיר לו אור השם ויבא על הענין ואדרבה בגילוי
אור ביותר.

וכן הוא בעבודה בתפילה שאי אפשר להיות השגה והתבוננות
טובה . . . להתפעל באהבה ויראה, כי אם בהקדם תחלה השפלות
ומרירות הנקרא כובד ראש.

Our Sages expounded on the verse, "Those who sow
with tears, reap with song." The song of reaping is
commensurate with the tears during sowing.

In material matters, such as business, one only profits
through intense effort to the point of feeling utterly
harried. He invests a great fortune—his own money,
as well as funds borrowed from others at exorbitant
interest rates. Sometimes he stands to lose everything.
He endures terrible anxiety, G-d forbid, from the many
obstacles and delays, suffering heartache and utter
despair. From the depths of his heart, he turns to G-d
in supplication, pleading for mercy to be spared. Only
then does G-d bring him success.

Likewise, in spiritual matters such as Torah study, it
is only accomplished through toil. . . . At times, one
suffers terrible pain and sadness, G-d forbid, from lack
of knowledge. He is terribly disgusted with himself to

the point that his heart and spirit break within him. And only then does he merit to be enlightened by G-d, and the matter is fully revealed to him.

Likewise, with respect to prayer, it is only from a sense of humility and remorse, described by our Sages as a reverent frame of mind, that we can be fully immersed in meditation that inspires love and fear of G-d.

TEXT 10

Talmud Tractate Berachot, 40a

כלי ריקן מחזיק, מלא אינו מחזיק.

An empty vessel can be filled, a full vessel cannot be filled.

TEXT 11

Talmud Tractate Eiruvin 13b

כל המשפיל עצמו, הקדוש ברוך הוא מגביהו, וכל המגביה עצמו הקדוש ברוך הוא משפילו.

G-d lifts those who lower themselves and lowers those who lift themselves.

TEXT 12

Zohar vol. 3 p. 195A

Zohar

The seminal work of kabbalah, Jewish mysticism. The *Zohar* is a mystical commentary on the Torah, written in Aramaic and Hebrew. According to the Arizal, the *Zohar* contains the teachings of Rabbi Shimon bar Yocha'i, who lived in the Land of Israel during the second century. The *Zohar* has become one of the indispensable texts of traditional Judaism, alongside and nearly equal in stature to the Mishnah and Talmud.

מאי חשיבא מכלהו?
הוי אימא תפלה דעני. תפילה דא קדים לתפלה דמשה, וקדים לתפלה דדוד, וקדים לכל שאר צלותין דעלמא. מאי טעמא?
בגין דעני איהו תבר ליבא... וקודשא בריך הוא אצית ושמע מלוי. כיון דצלי צלותיה, פצח כל כוי רקיעין וכל שאר צלותין דקא סלקא לעילא, דחי לון ההיא מסקנא תביר לבא... ולא עאלין עד דצלותא דיליה עאלת. וקודשא בריך הוא אמר, יתעטפון כל צלותין, וצלותא דא תיעול לגבעי. לא בעינא הכא בי דינא דידונון בינגא. קמאי ליהוו תרעומין דיליה ואנא והוא בלחודנא.

Which prayer is most important to G-d?

The prayer of the impoverished. It precedes the prayer of Moses and the prayer of David. It precedes all the prayers in the world.

Why?

Because the poor pray with a broken heart . . . and G-d listens and hears their prayer. When they pray, all the windows of heaven open, and all the other prayers that preceded it, are shunted aside for the prayer of the broken-hearted and poor. . . . They do not ascend before G-d until after the poor person's prayer has ascended. G-d proclaims, "Postpone all other prayers and bring this prayer before me. I do not want the celestial court to adjudicate between me and the poor. Bring these complaints directly to me; the poor and I shall be alone."

Ultimate Growth

Encounter with G-d

TEXT 13

The Rebbe, Torat Menachem, Sefer Hama'amarim 5726, p. 8

ועל פי זה יש לבאר ענין אמירת הפסוק, "מן המיצר קראתי גו'"
קודם תקיעת שופר, דאף שלאחרי העבודה דחודש אלול, ימי
הסליחות, ערב ראש השנה, ליל ראש השנה, עד לבוקר דראש
השנה לפני תקיעת שופר, בודאי נמצאים כבר במעמד ומצב של
יציאה מן המיצר. מכל מקום הרי זה עדיין בבחינת מיצר לגבי
דרגות נעלות יותר.

ובעומק יותר, שדוקא לאחרי היציאה מן המיצר שנעשית על ידי
הקדמת העבודה דחודש אלול כו' עד לבוקר דראש השנה לפני
תקיעת שופר, אזי באים להכרה שגם העבודה בדרגא היותר נעלית
היא עדיין בבחינת מיצר, שהרי לגבי עצמות אור אין סוף כולא קמי
כלא חשיב, ולית מחשבה תפיסא בי כלל, אפילו מחשבה דאדם
קדמון. אם כן, גם כאשר עבודתו היא בדרגא היותר נעלית, אינו
תופס מקום כלל. ומזה נעשה במיצר כו', ואומר באמת מן המיצר
קראתי גו'.

According to this, we can explain the meaning of the verse, "From the straits I call to G-d," which we chant before sounding the shofar on Rosh Hashanah. This is puzzling inasmuch as we are certainly "out of the straits" by the time we sound the shofar on Rosh Hashanah, considering that we have been drawing closer to G-d throughout the month of Elul. Add to that the days of supplication, the last day of the year—Erev Rosh Hashanah, the eve of Rosh Hashanah and the morning of Rosh Hashanah[—how can we be considered "in the straits?"]

We are, in fact, still in the straits relative to the higher levels we still wish to reach.

In fact, it is only through our work in the month of Elul and in the days leading up to Rosh Hashanah that we recognize that, despite the intense relationship with G-d that we have attained, we are still in the straits. As we draw closer to G-d, we realize that everything, even the highest level, is as naught before the essence of G-d. If so, we have achieved nothing despite our greatest efforts, and for this reason we feel constricted and cry out sincerely, "From the straits I call to G-d."

TEXT 14

Ibid., pp. 10–11

אך הענין הוא, דהזמן שהחדש מתכסה בו הוא הרגע שלפני המולד, שהרי ברגע המולד ישנה מציאות הלבנה באופן של נקודה על כל פנים. וענין הכיסוי הוא ברגע שלפני המולד, שהוא באופן של העדר המציאות לגמרי, אפילו לא מציאות באופן של נקודה בלבד. וזהו שתלה הכתוב היום טוב דראש השנה במה שההחדש מתכסה בו, שהוא ענין העדר המציאות לגמרי. . . וכן הוא גם בענין המיצר דראש השנה קודם תקיעת שופר שהוא באופן של העדר המציאות לגמרי, אפילו לא מציאות באופן של נקודה בלבד. שזהו מצד הגילוי דעצמות אור אין סוף, שכולא קמיה כלא חשיב, באופן של העדר המציאות לגמרי.

Just before the moon is reborn at the beginning of the month, it is completely concealed for but a moment. When it is reborn, a tiny sliver becomes visible, but the moment before its rebirth, it is as if it were nonexistent.

Rosh Hashanah begins when the moon is concealed, because the straits that we experience on Rosh Hashanah just before we sound the shofar are akin to the feeling of being completely nonexistent. We feel as if we are utterly nonexistent because we come face to face with the essence of G-d's infinite light before whom all is naught.

The Inarticulate Call of the Shofar

TEXT 15

Rabbi Shneur Zalman of Liadi, Likutei Torah, Rosh Hashanah, 54B

Rabbi Shne'ur Zalman of Liadi
(Alter Rebbe)
1745–1812
Chasidic rebbe, halachic authority, and founder of the Chabad movement. The Alter Rebbe was born in Liozna, Belarus, and was among the principal students of the Magid of Mezeritch. His numerous works include the *Tanya*, an early classic containing the fundamentals of Chabad Chasidism, and *Shulchan Aruch Harav*, an expanded and reworked code of Jewish law.

"תקעו בחדש שופר . . . חגנו," פירוש תקעו. תקיעה הוא קול פשוט
היוצא מהבל הלב, מפנימיותו. והוא בחינת צעקת הלב היוצאת
מפנימית הלב שלמעלה מעלה מהחכמה שאי אפשר להוציא
בשפתיו בדיבור. . . ועל זה נאמר, "שמעה בקולי," פירוש בקולי -
מה שבתוך קולי, דהיינו תוכיותו ופנימיותו, שהוא בחינת פנימיות
הלב. . . המתגלה בבחינת שופר.

"Sound the Shofar on the new moon." This sound refers to the inarticulate cry that emerges from the very depths of the heart. The heart's cry from its very depths transcends the intellect and cannot be articulated in speech. It is with respect to this cry that it is written, "Hearken in my voice," in my voice refers to a message that is deeply embedded within my voice. This is the wordless call of the shofar that reveals the depth of the heart.

11

Jews in Shoes

Grounded Below, Turned Above

*Dedicated by **Anonymous** to the success of the **Torah Studies** team.*

OVERVIEW
Yom Kippur

Yom Kippur is the holiest day of the year—the day on which we are closest to G-d and to the quintessence of our own souls. It is the Day of Atonement—"For on this day He will forgive you, to purify you, that you be cleansed from all your sins before G-d" (Leviticus 16:30).

For nearly twenty-six hours—from several minutes before sunset on 9 Tishrei to after nightfall on 10 Tishrei—we "afflict our souls": we abstain from food and drink, do not wash or anoint our bodies, do not wear leather footwear, and abstain from marital relations.

Before Yom Kippur we perform the kaparot *atonement service; we request and receive honey cake, in acknowledgement that we are all recipients in G-d's world, and in prayerful hope for a sweet and abundant year; eat a festive meal; immerse in a* mikvah; *and give extra charity. In the late afternoon we eat the pre-fast meal, following which we bless our children, light a memorial candle as well as the holiday candles, and go to the synagogue for the Kol Nidrei service.*

In the course of Yom Kippur we hold five prayer servic-es: Maariv, *with its solemn* Kol Nidrei *service, on the eve of Yom Kippur;* Shacharit—*the morning prayer, which includes a reading from Leviticus followed by the* Yizkor *memorial service;* Musaf, *which includes a detailed account of the Yom Kippur Temple service;* Minchah, *which includes the reading of the Book of Jonah; and* Neilah, *the "closing of the gates" service at sunset. We say the* Al Chet *confession of sins eight times in the course of Yom Kippur, and recite Psalms every available moment.*

The day is the most solemn of the year, yet an under-tone of joy suffuses it: a joy that revels in the spirituality of the day and expresses the confidence that G-d will accept our repentance, forgive our sins, and seal our verdict for a year of life, health and happiness. The closing Neilah *service climaxes in the resounding cries of "Hear O Israel . . . G-d is one." Then joy erupts in song and dance (a Chabad custom is to sing the lively "Napoleon's March"), followed by a single blast of the* shofar, *followed by the proclamation, "Next year in Jerusalem." We then partake of a festive after-fast meal, making the evening after Yom Kippur a* yom tov *(festival) in its own right.*

Kick-Off

Yom Kippur by the Book

TEXT 1

Vayikra (Leviticus) 23:26–32

וַיְדַבֵּר ה' אֶל מֹשֶׁה לֵּאמֹר.

אַךְ בֶּעָשׂוֹר לַחֹדֶשׁ הַשְּׁבִיעִי הַזֶּה יוֹם הַכִּפֻּרִים הוּא מִקְרָא קֹדֶשׁ יִהְיֶה לָכֶם וְעִנִּיתֶם אֶת נַפְשֹׁתֵיכֶם וְהִקְרַבְתֶּם אִשֶּׁה לַה'.

וְכָל מְלָאכָה לֹא תַעֲשׂוּ בְּעֶצֶם הַיּוֹם הַזֶּה כִּי יוֹם כִּפֻּרִים הוּא לְכַפֵּר עֲלֵיכֶם לִפְנֵי ה' אֱלֹקֵיכֶם.

כִּי כָל הַנֶּפֶשׁ אֲשֶׁר לֹא תְעֻנֶּה בְּעֶצֶם הַיּוֹם הַזֶּה וְנִכְרְתָה מֵעַמֶּיהָ.

וְכָל הַנֶּפֶשׁ אֲשֶׁר תַּעֲשֶׂה כָּל מְלָאכָה בְּעֶצֶם הַיּוֹם הַזֶּה וְהַאֲבַדְתִּי אֶת הַנֶּפֶשׁ הַהִוא מִקֶּרֶב עַמָּהּ.

כָּל מְלָאכָה לֹא תַעֲשׂוּ חֻקַּת עוֹלָם לְדֹרֹתֵיכֶם בְּכֹל מֹשְׁבֹתֵיכֶם.

שַׁבַּת שַׁבָּתוֹן הוּא לָכֶם וְעִנִּיתֶם אֶת נַפְשֹׁתֵיכֶם בְּתִשְׁעָה לַחֹדֶשׁ בָּעֶרֶב מֵעֶרֶב עַד עֶרֶב תִּשְׁבְּתוּ שַׁבַּתְּכֶם.

And G-d spoke to Moses, saying:

But on the tenth of this seventh month, it is a day of atonement, it shall be a holy occasion for you; you shall afflict yourselves, and you shall offer up a fire offering to G-d.

You shall not perform any work on that very day, for it is a day of atonement, for you to gain atonement before the Lord, your G-d.

For any person who will not be afflicted on that very day shall be cut off from its people.

And any person who performs any work on that very day, I will destroy that person from amidst its people.

You shall not perform any work. [This is] an eternal statute throughout your generations in all your dwelling places.

It is a complete day of rest for you, and you shall afflict yourselves. On the ninth of the month in the evening, from evening to evening, you shall observe your rest day.

Atonement and Affliction

TEXT 2

Maimonides Mishneh Torah, Hilchot Shevisat Asor 1:4–5

Rabbi Moshe ben Maimon
(Maimonides, Rambam)
1135–1204

Halachist, philosopher, author, and physician. Maimonides was born in Córdoba, Spain. After the conquest of Córdoba by the Almohads, he fled Spain and eventually settled in Cairo, Egypt. There, he became the leader of the Jewish community and served as court physician to the vizier of Egypt. He is most noted for authoring the *Mishneh Torah*, an encyclopedic arrangement of Jewish law, and for his philosophical work, *Guide for the Perplexed*. His rulings on Jewish law are integral to the formation of halachic consensus.

מצות עשה אחרת יש ביום הכפורים והיא לשבות בו מאכילה ושתיה שנאמר תענו את נפשותיכם. מפי השמועה למדו אי זה הוא ענוי שהוא לנפש זה הצום.

וכל הצם בו קיים מצות עשה. וכל האוכל ושותה בו בטל מצות עשה ועבר על לא תעשה שנאמר כי כל הנפש אשר לא תעונה בעצם היום הזה ונכרתה. . .

וכן למדנו מפי השמועה שאסור לרחוץ בו או לסוך בו או לנעול את הסנדל או לבעול.

There is another positive commandment on Yom Kippur, to refrain from eating and drinking, as is stated, "You shall afflict your souls." According to the Oral Tradition, it has been taught: What is meant by afflicting one's soul? –fasting.

Whoever fasts on this day fulfills a positive commandment. Whoever eats or drinks on this day negates the observance of [this] positive commandment and violates a negative commandment, as it is stated, "Any soul that does not afflict itself will be cut off.". . .

Similarly, according to the Oral Tradition, it has been taught that it is forbidden to wash, anoint oneself, wear shoes, or engage in sexual relations on this day. It *is a mitzvah to refrain from these activities in the same way one refrains from eating and drinking.*

The Mitzvah of Fasting on the Tenth of Tishrei

TEXT 3

Sefer Hachinuch, Mitzvah 313

משרשי המצוה. שהיה מחסדי השם על כל בריותיו לקבע להם יום אחד בשנה לכפר על החטאים עם התשובה, וכמו שכתבתי באורכה בסדר אחרי מות במצות עבודת יום הכפורים.

ולכן נצטוינו להתענות בו, לפי שהמאכל והמשתה ויתר הנאות חוש המשוש, יעוררו החומר להמשך אחר התאוה והחטא, ויבטלו צורת הנפש החכמה מחפש אחר האמת שהוא עבודת הא-ל ומוסרו הטוב והמתוק לכל בני הדעת.

ואין ראוי לעשות ביום בואו לדין לפני אדוניו לבוא בנפש חשוכה ומערבבת מתוך המאכל והמשתה במחשבות החומר אשר היא בתוכו, שאין דנין את האדם אלא לפי מעשיו שבאותה שעה, על כן טוב לו להגביר נפשו החכמה ולהכניע החומר לפניה באותו היום הנכבד, למען תהיה ראויה ונכונה לקבל כפרתה, ולא ימנענה מסך התאוות.

Sefer Hachinuch
A work on the biblical commandments. Four aspects of every mitzvah are discussed in this work: the definition of the mitzvah; ethical lessons that can be deduced from the mitzvah; basic laws pertaining to the observance of the mitzvah; and who is obligated to perform the mitzvah, and when. The work was composed in the 13th century by an anonymous author who refers to himself as "the Levite of Barcelona." It has been widely thought that this referred to Rabbi Aharon Halevi of Barcelona (Re'ah); however, this view has been contested.

The message of this mitzvah is: Out of His kindness towards His creatures, G-d established one day in the year to atone for their sins through repentance, as I wrote at length in the parasha *of Achrei Mot, regarding the commandment of the Yom Kippur service.*

Therefore we were commanded to fast on this day, as food and drink and the other sensual pleasures propel the corporeal self toward desire and sin and thwart the wise soul's search for the truth—which is the service of G-d and His ethics, [which are] good and sweet for anyone with knowledge.

[Such conduct] it is not fitting on the day one comes to judgement in front of his Master; to come with a soul dimmed and distracted by food and drink, with thoughts of the material which is in it. Inasmuch as a person is judged according to his deeds at that time, it is good for him to strengthen his wise soul and to subdue the corporeal before it on this glorious day, so that [the soul] will be worthy and ready to receive atonement, and [that] the veil of desires not prevent it.

No Shoes, No Services?

TEXT 4

Rabbi Shneur Zalman of Liadi, Shulchan Aruch Harav, Orach Chaim 614:2–3

Rabbi Shneur Zalman of Liadi
(Alter Rebbe)
1745–1812
Chasidic rebbe, halachic authority, and founder of the Chabad movement. The Alter Rebbe was born in Liozna, Belarus, and was among the principal students of the Magid of Mezeritch. His numerous works include the *Tanya*, an early classic containing the fundamentals of Chabad Chasidism, and *Shulchan Aruch Harav*, an expanded and reworked code of Jewish law.

נעילת הסנדל כיצד?

אסור לנעול מנעל של עור וסנדל של עור אפילו ברגלו אחת ואין
חילוק בין ביתו לרשות הרבים בכל מקום אסור ...
אבל מותר לנעול סנדל או מנעל של גמי ושל קש ושל בגד או
של שאר מינים שהרי גושי הארץ מגיע לרגליו ומרגיש שהוא יחף
ועוד שלא אסרו אלא מנעל וכל שאינו של עור אינו נקרא מנעל
אלא מלבוש.

What does [the prohibition against] wearing shoes entail? It is forbidden to wear leather shoes or leather sandals, even on one foot, regardless of whether one is at home or in the public domain. The prohibition applies everywhere. It is even forbidden to wear a wooden shoe that is lined with leather. If possible, one should be stringent and not wear a wooden shoe, even if it is not lined with leather . . .

It is, however, permissible to wear sandals or shoes made of reeds, straw, cloth, or other substances, because [then] one's feet feel the bumps on the ground; [indeed,] he feels as if he is barefoot. Moreover, [the Sages] forbade only a shoe, and [a foot-covering] that is not made of leather is considered a garment, not a shoe.

Just for Kicks

TEXT 5

Rabbi Shenur Zalman of Liadi, Shulchan
Aruch Harav Orach Chaim 46:2

ברכות השחר נתקנו לברך כל אחת בשעה שנתחייב בה.
דהיינו כשיעור משנתו יאמר: אלקי נשמה, וכששומע קול התרנגול
יברך הנותן לשכוי בינה, וכשלובש חלוקו והוא מושכב יברך מלביש
ערומים, וכשמניח ידו על עיניו דרך חלוק . . . יברך פוקח עורים,
וכשיושב יברך מתיר אסורים, מפני שמניע עצמותיו שהיו כל
הלילה כמו כפותים, וכשזוקף יברך זוקף כפופים, שהיתה קומתו
כפופה כל הלילה ועכשיו עמדה על מעמדה, וכשמניח רגליו בארץ
יברך רוקע הארץ על המים.
וכשנועל מנעליו יברך שעשה לי כל צרכי. ואין לשנות הנוסח ולומר
צרכי הכ״ף בקמץ שהוא לשון רבים מפני שברכה זו אינו אלא על
נעילת מנעלים שהוא צורך האדם.

*[Initially, the Sages] ordained that each of the Morning
Blessings should be recited at the time its obligation is
incurred. Thus, when one wakes from sleep he should
say* e-lohai neshamah. *When he hears a rooster crow,
he should recite the blessing* hanosen lasechvi binah.
*When he puts on his shirt, while lying down, he should
recite the blessing* malbish arumim. *When he touches
his eyes, using his shirt as a buffer, he should recite the
blessing* pokeiach ivrim . . .

When he sits up, he should recite the blessing matir asurim, *for he is moving his limbs which were as if fettered the entire night. When he stands up, he should recite the blessing* zokeif kefufim, *for his body was bent over throughout the night and is now standing upright. When he places his feet on the ground, he should recite the blessing* roka haaretz al hamayim.

When he puts on his shoes, he should recite the blessing sheasah li kol tzorki *("Who has provided me with all I need"). One should not alter the wording of the blessing and use the plural form—*tzrachai, *reading the* chaf *with a* kamatz *("all of my needs")— because this blessing refers only to the wearing of shoes, which is a necessity for man. (As to the fulfillment of one's other needs, one recites a separate blessing for each of them when he enjoys the relevant benefit.)*

TEXT 6

Rabbi Shneur Zalman of Liadi Siddur, Morning Blessings

בתשעה באב וביום הכיפורים אין אומרים ברכה זו.

On the Ninth of Av and Yom Kippur, we do not say this blessing.

Swords, Sandals, and Scripture

Hallowed Space, Hallowed Time

TEXT 7

Shemos (Exodus) 3:1–5

וּמֹשֶׁה הָיָה רֹעֶה אֶת צֹאן יִתְרוֹ חֹתְנוֹ כֹּהֵן מִדְיָן וַיִּנְהַג אֶת הַצֹּאן אַחַר
הַמִּדְבָּר וַיָּבֹא אֶל הַר הָאֱלֹקִים חֹרֵבָה:

וַיֵּרָא מַלְאַךְ ה' אֵלָיו בְּלַבַּת אֵשׁ מִתּוֹךְ הַסְּנֶה וַיַּרְא וְהִנֵּה הַסְּנֶה בֹּעֵר
בָּאֵשׁ וְהַסְּנֶה אֵינֶנּוּ אֻכָּל:

וַיֹּאמֶר מֹשֶׁה אָסֻרָה נָּא וְאֶרְאֶה אֶת הַמַּרְאֶה הַגָּדֹל הַזֶּה מַדּוּעַ לֹא
יִבְעַר הַסְּנֶה:

וַיַּרְא ה' כִּי סָר לִרְאוֹת וַיִּקְרָא אֵלָיו אֱלֹהִים מִתּוֹךְ הַסְּנֶה וַיֹּאמֶר מֹשֶׁה
מֹשֶׁה וַיֹּאמֶר הִנֵּנִי:

וַיֹּאמֶר אַל תִּקְרַב הֲלֹם שַׁל נְעָלֶיךָ מֵעַל רַגְלֶיךָ כִּי הַמָּקוֹם אֲשֶׁר אַתָּה
עוֹמֵד עָלָיו אַדְמַת קֹדֶשׁ הוּא:

Moses was pasturing the flocks of Jethro, his father-in-law, the chief of Midian, and he led the flocks after the free pastureland, and he came to the mountain of G-d, to Horeb.

An angel of G-d appeared to him in a flame of fire from within the thorn bush, and behold, the thorn bush was burning with fire, but the thorn bush was not being consumed.

So Moses said, "Let me turn now and see this great spectacle; Why does the thorn bush not burn up?"

G-d saw that he had turned to see, and G-d called to him from within the thorn bush, and He said, "Moses, Moses!" And he said, "Here I am!"

And He said, "Do not draw near here. Take your shoes off your feet, because the place upon which you stand is holy soil."

Everything but the Shoes

TEXT 8

Maimonides, Mishneh Torah, Hilchos Beit Hamikdash, 5:17

וכן כל העוסק בעבודה מעבודת המקדש צריך שיהיה עומד על הרצפה ואם היה דבר חוצץ בינו ובין הקרקע כגון שעמד על גבי כלים או בהמה או על רגלי חבירו פסל וכן אם היה דבר חוצץ בין ידו ובין הכלי שעובד בו פסל.

Similarly, anyone involved with one of the Temple services must be standing on the floor. If there was anything intervening between himself and the ground, e.g., he was standing on a utensil, an animal, or a colleague's foot, [his service] is invalid.

Similarly, if there was anything intervening between his hand and the utensil with which he was performing the service, it is invalid.

Not only was this true of the attendants working in the Temple, but also of anyone who stepped foot onto the Temple Mount. Even for those to whom the priestly dress code did not apply, the no-shoes rule still held, as the Mishna itself makes clear:

TEXT 9

Mishnah Tractate Brachot 9:5

Mishnah
The first authoritative work of Jewish law that was codified in writing. The Mishnah contains the oral traditions that were passed down from teacher to student; it supplements, clarifies, and systematizes the commandments of the Torah. Due to the continual persecution of the Jewish people, it became increasingly difficult to guarantee that these traditions would not be forgotten. Rabbi Yehudah Hanasi therefore redacted the Mishnah at the end of the second century. It serves as the foundation for the Talmud.

ולא יכנס להר הבית במקלו ובמנעלו ובפונדתו ובאבק שעל רגליו.

One may not enter the Temple Mount with his staff, while wearing shoes, with his money belt, or with the dust on his feet.

TEXT 10

Midrash Rabah, Shemot, 2:6

"שֶׁל נְעָלֶיךָ" — כָּל מָקוֹם שֶׁהַשְּׁכִינָה נִגְלֵית אָסוּר בִּנְעִילַת הַסַּנְדָּל,
וְכֵן בִּיהוֹשֻׁעַ "שַׁל נְעָלְךָ", וְכֵן הַכֹּהֲנִים לֹא שִׁמְּשׁוּ בְמִקְדָּשׁ אֶלָּא יְחֵפִים.

"Remove your shoes." In any place the divine presence is revealed, there is a prohibition against wearing shoes.

So it was with Joshua, [who was similarly instructed to] "remove your shoe," and so it was that the priests would only perform the Temple service barefoot.

Shemot Rabah

An early rabbinic commentary on the Book of Exodus. Midrash is the designation of a particular genre of rabbinic literature usually forming a running commentary on specific books of the Bible. *Shemot Rabah*, written mostly in Hebrew, provides textual exegeses, expounds upon the biblical narrative, and develops and illustrates moral principles. It was first printed in Constantinople in 1512 together with four other Midrashic works on the other four books of the Pentateuch.

On One Foot

TEXT 11

Talmud Tractate Chulin 24b

יֶלֶד עַד כַּמָּה?
אָמַר רַבִּי אֶלְעָא אָמַר רַבִּי חֲנִינָא: כָּל שֶׁעוֹמֵד עַל רַגְלוֹ אַחַת וְחוֹלֵץ
מִנְעָלוֹ וְנוֹעֵל מִנְעָלוֹ. אָמְרוּ עָלָיו עַל רַבִּי חֲנִינָא, שֶׁהָיָה בֶּן שְׁמוֹנִים
שָׁנָה וְהָיָה עוֹמֵד עַל רַגְלוֹ אַחַת וְחוֹלֵץ מִנְעָלוֹ וְנוֹעֵל מִנְעָלוֹ.

How long [is one regarded as young and healthy]?— Rabbi Ila'a said in the name of Rabbi Chanina: As long as one is able to stand on one foot and put on and take off one's shoe. It was said of Rabbi Chanina that at the age of eighty years he was able to stand on one foot

Babylonian Talmud

A literary work of monumental proportions that draws upon the legal, spiritual, intellectual, ethical, and historical traditions of Judaism. The 37 tractates of the Babylonian Talmud contain the teachings of the Jewish Sages from the period after the destruction of the Second Temple through the fifth century CE. It has served as the primary vehicle for the transmission of the Oral Law and the education of Jews over the centuries; it is the entry point for all subsequent legal, ethical, and theological Jewish scholarship.

and put on and take off his shoe. *Rabbi Chanina said: The warm baths and the oil with which my mother anointed me in my youth have stood me in good stead in my old age.*

Following the Shoeprints

TEXT 12A

Yeshayahu (Isaiah) 11:1–9

וְיָצָא חֹטֶר מִגֶּזַע יִשָׁי וְנֵצֶר מִשָּׁרָשָׁיו יִפְרֶה.

וְנָחָה עָלָיו רוּחַ ה' רוּחַ חָכְמָה וּבִינָה רוּחַ עֵצָה וּגְבוּרָה רוּחַ דַּעַת וְיִרְאַת ה'.

וַהֲרִיחוֹ בְּיִרְאַת ה' וְלֹא לְמַרְאֵה עֵינָיו יִשְׁפּוֹט וְלֹא לְמִשְׁמַע אָזְנָיו יוֹכִיחַ.

וְשָׁפַט בְּצֶדֶק דַּלִּים וְהוֹכִיחַ בְּמִישׁוֹר לְעַנְוֵי אָרֶץ וְהִכָּה אֶרֶץ בְּשֵׁבֶט פִּיו וּבְרוּחַ שְׂפָתָיו יָמִית רָשָׁע

וְהָיָה צֶדֶק אֵזוֹר מָתְנָיו וְהָאֱמוּנָה אֵזוֹר חֲלָצָיו. וְגָר זְאֵב עִם כֶּבֶשׂ וְנָמֵר עִם גְּדִי יִרְבָּץ וְעֵגֶל וּכְפִיר וּמְרִיא יַחְדָּו וְנַעַר קָטֹן נֹהֵג בָּם.

וּפָרָה וָדֹב תִּרְעֶינָה יַחְדָּו יִרְבְּצוּ יַלְדֵיהֶן וְאַרְיֵה כַּבָּקָר יֹאכַל תֶּבֶן.

וְשִׁעֲשַׁע יוֹנֵק עַל חֻר פָּתֶן וְעַל מְאוּרַת צִפְעוֹנִי גָּמוּל יָדוֹ הָדָה. לֹא יָרֵעוּ וְלֹא יַשְׁחִיתוּ בְּכָל הַר קָדְשִׁי כִּי מָלְאָה הָאָרֶץ דֵּעָה אֶת ה' כַּמַּיִם לַיָּם מְכַסִּים.

And a shoot shall spring forth from the stem of Jesse, and a twig shall sprout from his roots.

And the spirit of G-d shall rest upon him, a spirit of wisdom and understanding, a spirit of counsel and heroism, a spirit of knowledge and fear of G-d.

And he shall be animated by the fear of G-d, and neither with the sight of his eyes shall he judge, nor with the hearing of his ears shall he chastise.

And he shall judge the poor justly, and he shall chastise with equity the humble of the earth, and he shall smite the earth with the rod of his mouth and with the breath of his lips he shall put the wicked to death.

And righteousness shall be the girdle of his loins and faith the girdle of his loins. And a wolf shall live with a lamb, and a leopard shall lie with a kid; and a calf and a lion cub and a fatling [shall lie] together, and a small child shall lead them.

And a cow and a bear shall graze together, their children shall lie; and a lion, like cattle, shall eat straw.

And an infant shall play over the hole of an old snake and over the eyeball of an adder, a weaned child shall stretch forth his hand. They shall neither harm nor destroy on all My holy mount, for the land shall be full of knowledge of G-d as water covers the sea bed.

TEXT 12B

Yeshayahu (Isaiah) 11:11–16

וְהָיָה בַּיּוֹם הַהוּא יוֹסִיף אֲ-דֹנָי שֵׁנִית יָדוֹ לִקְנוֹת אֶת שְׁאָר עַמּוֹ אֲשֶׁר
יִשָּׁאֵר מֵאַשּׁוּר וּמִמִּצְרַיִם וּמִפַּתְרוֹס וּמִכּוּשׁ וּמֵעֵילָם וּמִשִּׁנְעָר וּמֵחֲמָת
וּמֵאִיֵּי הַיָּם.

וְנָשָׂא נֵס לַגּוֹיִם וְאָסַף נִדְחֵי יִשְׂרָאֵל וּנְפֻצוֹת יְהוּדָה יְקַבֵּץ מֵאַרְבַּע
כַּנְפוֹת הָאָרֶץ.

וְסָרָה קִנְאַת אֶפְרַיִם וְצֹרְרֵי יְהוּדָה יִכָּרֵתוּ אֶפְרַיִם לֹא יְקַנֵּא אֶת יְהוּדָה
וִיהוּדָה לֹא יָצֹר אֶת אֶפְרָיִם.

וְעָפוּ בְכָתֵף פְּלִשְׁתִּים יָמָּה יַחְדָּו יָבֹזּוּ אֶת בְּנֵי קֶדֶם אֱדוֹם וּמוֹאָב
מִשְׁלוֹחַ יָדָם וּבְנֵי עַמּוֹן מִשְׁמַעְתָּם.

וְהֶחֱרִים ה' אֵת לְשׁוֹן יָם מִצְרַיִם וְהֵנִיף יָדוֹ עַל הַנָּהָר בַּעְיָם רוּחוֹ וְהִכָּהוּ
לְשִׁבְעָה נְחָלִים וְהִדְרִיךְ בַּנְּעָלִים.

וְהָיְתָה מְסִלָּה לִשְׁאָר עַמּוֹ אֲשֶׁר יִשָּׁאֵר מֵאַשּׁוּר כַּאֲשֶׁר הָיְתָה לְיִשְׂרָאֵל
בְּיוֹם עֲלֹתוֹ מֵאֶרֶץ מִצְרָיִם.

And it shall come to pass that on that day, G-d shall continue to apply His hand a second time to acquire the rest of His people that will remain from Assyria and from Egypt and from Pathros and from Cush and from Elam and from Sumeria and from Hamath and from the islands of the sea.

And He shall raise a banner to the nations, and He shall gather the lost of Israel, and the scattered ones of Judah He shall gather from the four corners of the earth.

And the envy of Ephraim shall cease, and the adversaries of Judah shall be cut off; Ephraim shall not envy Judah, nor shall Judah vex Ephraim.

And they shall fly of one accord against the Philistines in the west, together they shall plunder the children of the East; upon Edom and Moab shall they stretch forth their hand, and the children of Ammon shall obey them.

And G-d shall dry up the tongue of the Egyptian Sea, and He shall lift His hand over the river with the strength of His wind, and He shall beat it into seven streams, and He shall lead [the exiles] with shoes.

And there shall be a highway for the remnant of His people who remain from Assyria, as there was for Israel on the day they went up from the land of Egypt.

Tying it all Together: The Secret of Shoes

A Sole Comes Down to the Earth

TEXT 13

Rabbi Levi Yitzchak Schneerson, Likutei Levi Yitzchak, vol. 3, Igrot Kodesh, p. 387

Thank you for the shoes, which made it in time for the holiday of Passover/Pesach.

(In reference to which it is written [in Exodus (Shemot) 12:11, that the Korbon Pesach *should be eaten with] "your shoes on your feet"; as in the future redemption, when "He will lead with shoes." So it is written [Shir Hashirim 7:2], "How beautiful are your feet in sandals, O daughter of nobles [bas nediv]," which is a reference to the daughter [bas] of Abraham, who is called "generous" [nediv]. Abraham is especially connected with Pesach; it is the first holiday and is associated with kindness [the first of the divine emotional attributes]; just as he is the first forefather, and associated with kindness; he rejected the shoe of the king of Sodom, as it is written [in Genesis (Bereishit) 14:23, when he refuses to accept any spoils of war, including] "even*

a shoe lace"; rather, the shoes must be of the realm of holiness; it is these that will bring about the downfall of the nations, as it is written [Psalms (Tehilim) 108:10], "on Edom I cast my shoe"; here is not the place to elaborate, and this will suffice for the understanding.)

TEXT 14

The Lubavitcher Rebbe, Hama'or ShebeTorah, Shemot, p. 37

משמעותן של נעליים היא יצירת חציצה והפסק בין האדם ובין האדמה, הארציות והחומריות.

ראשו של האדם–הוא מטבעו גבוה ומובדל מן הארץ, שכן האיברים והכוחות הנעלים שבאדם הם מטבעם נעלים ורחוקים מחומריות; אבל החלק התחתון שבאדם–הרגל–הוא מטבעו קרוב לארץ, ונוטה לעניינים ארציים וחומריים.

ולכן יש צורך לנעול נעליים, כדי ליצור הפסק גם בין החלק התחתון שבאדם ובין הארץ, כדי שגם חלק זה שבאדם לא ישקע לגמרי בתוך הארציות והחומריות.

כל זאת–כשמדובר במקום של חולין. אבל כאשר מדובר ב"אדמת קודש" –אין צורך לחצוץ בין האדם ובין האדמה; אדרבה–במקום כזה על האדם ללכת יחף דוקא, שלא תהיה חציצה בינו ובין הקודש.

Rabbi Menachem Mendel Schneerson
1902–1994

The towering Jewish leader of the 20th century, known as "the Lubavitcher Rebbe," or simply as "the Rebbe." Born in southern Ukraine, the Rebbe escaped Nazi-occupied Europe, arriving in the U.S. in June 1941. The Rebbe inspired and guided the revival of traditional Judaism after the European devastation, impacting virtually every Jewish community the world over. The Rebbe often emphasized that the performance of just one additional good deed could usher in the era of Mashiach. The Rebbe's scholarly talks and writings have been printed in more than 200 volumes.

Shoes represent the creation of a barrier or buffer between man and the ground, earthiness, and materiality.

A person's head is naturally higher and removed from the earth, just as one's upper limbs and superior *faculties are naturally at a loftier level removed from the material. However, the lower part of one's body, that is the feet, is naturally closer to the earth, and tends to earthy, material things.*

Therefore, there is a need to don shoes, in order to create an interruption between even the lower part of man and the earth, so that even this part within man does not sink entirely into earthiness and the material.

All of this is so with regards to the profane. However, when in the presence of "holy ground," there is no need to intervene between the person and the ground. On the contrary: in such a place, one ought specifically to go barefoot, so that there should be no barrier between him or her, and the ground.

Not Just Affliction

TEXT 15

The Rebbe, Reshimat Hamenorah, pp. 91–3

ששת ימי המעשה, שאז הוא זמן ד"ואספת את דגנך", וצריך אזהרה "השמרו לכם פן יפתה לבבכם וסרתם וגו'". שבת, ד"ושמרתם את השבת כי קדש היא", ואז ל"ט מלאכות אסורות, בורר אסור. וגם הגולם נזדכך . . אבל בכל זה מצוה לענגו באכילה ושתיה . . מה שאין כן ביום הכפורים שאז דומים כמלאכים . . ואין אכילה ושתיה, ונעילת הסנדל אסורה, כי צריך להיות "של נעליך", כיון שהוא יום קדוש ה'.

During the six days of world activity, during the time when [as it states in the second part of Shema] "you gather up the harvest," there is a need for the precaution [as the verse continues], "take care, lest your heart be misled, and you turn away."

Shabbat is a time when "you must guard that Shabbos, for it is holy," [one minimizes engagement with the world, so that] the thirty-nine categories of weekday work are forbidden—including the prohibition against sorting good and bad—and even the very matter of the world is refined . . . Nevertheless, [even on Shabbos,] it is a mitzvah to indulge the day with eating and drinking. However, on Yom Kippur, when one resembles the angels . . . and there is no eating and drinking, and wearing shoes is prohibited—rather one must "remove your shoes," for the day is holy unto G-d.

TEXT 16

Shulchan Aruch Harav, Orach Chaim 610:9

יש נוהגין ללבוש בגדים לבנים נקיים ביום הכיפורים כדי להיות דוגמת מלאכי השרת, וכן נוהגין במדינות אלו ללבוש הקיטל שהוא בגד לבן ונקי.

It is the custom of some people to wear clean, white clothes on Yom Kippur to resemble the ministering angels. Indeed, the custom in these countries is to wear a kittel, *which is a clean, white garment.*

Paradise Lost and Found

TEXT 17A

The Lubavitcher Rebbe, Sichot Kodesh 5733, Acharon Shel Pesach §6

The fact that it was specifically shoes [that the angels found] seems to have been made an integral part of the story. Seemingly, one could just as have simply said that clothing or other out-of-place articles were found in Gan Eden; of what relevance is it that shoes were found? Had they found a hat, they could have wondered just the same: "What's a hat doing in Gan Eden?" It seems, therefore, that there is a deliberate emphasis on shoes here.

TEXT 17B

Ibid.

The difference between a [hat and a shoe] is that the concept of a hat bears obvious relevance in the upper spiritual realm: wearing a hat on one's head inspires the fear of Heaven, for example. The same is true for any other garment, each of which has a spiritual counterpart. Everything, that is, except shoes, which are designed and made for the simple purpose of shielding against the thorns and other sharp ends underfoot. Such a thing cannot exist in the spiritual realm, since in Gan Eden, the concept of a harmful "thorn" or "thistle" is moot . . .

The explanation [of the story], then, is this:

When one uses a shoe [for a positive purpose, like dancing on Simchat Torah], it is completely transforming it into a positive thing, so that the shoe arrives at its ultimate, ideal state: Inasmuch as "G-d did not create anything in His world for naught," every single thing must be brought to a state of perfection; the inanimate realm is perfected when it is transformed into the vegetative; the vegetative as it comes into the animal; the animal as it comes into man. The perfection of any creation is to become Creator; this is what happens with a Jew, when he learns Torah, for Israel becomes one with G-d through the Torah.

Likewise, when a Jew makes the holiday-pilgrimage to the Beit Hamikdash, on foot, he elevates his very shoes; he affects this elevation in every realm, bring each one to their perfection, to become one with G-d.

These Boots are Frayed from Working

TEXT 17C

Ibid.

For this same reason does it say, "He shall lead [the exiles] with shoes," which is to say even with their shoes, even the mostly lowly garment, will "cross over the river" along with the Jewish people.

12

Don't Kick the Sukkah

Religion Isn't Just about Feeling Good

*Dedicated to **Elliot Brown** in appreciation of his partnership in bringing the light of Torah to communities around the globe.*

OVERVIEW
Sukkot

For forty years, as our ancestors traversed the Sinai Desert, following the Exodus from Egypt, miraculous "Clouds of Glory" surrounded and hovered over them, shielding them from the dangers and discomforts of the desert. Ever since, we remember G-d's kindness and reaffirm our trust in His providence by dwelling in a sukkah—a hut of temporary construction with a roof covering of branches—for the duration of the Sukkot festival (on the Jewish calendar Tishrei 15–21). For seven days and nights we eat all our meals in the sukkah and otherwise regard it as our home.

Another Sukkot observance is the taking of the Four Kinds: an etrog (citron), a lulav (palm frond), three hadassim (myrtle twigs) and two aravot (willow twigs). On each day of the festival (excepting Shabbat), we take the Four Kinds, recite a blessing over them, bring them together in our hands, and wave them in all six directions: right, left, forward, up, down, and backward. Our Sages in the Midrash tell us that the Four Kinds represent the various types and personalities that comprise the community of Israel, whose intrinsic unity we emphasize on Sukkot.

Sukkot is also called The Time of Our Joy; indeed, a special joy pervades the festival. Nightly Water-Drawing Celebrations, reminiscent of the evening-to-dawn festivities held in the Holy Temple in preparation for the drawing of water for use in the festival service, fill the synagogues and streets with song, music, and dance until the wee hours of the morning.

The seventh day of Sukkot is called Hoshana Rabbah ("Great Salvation") and closes the period of Divine judgment begun on Rosh Hashanah. A special observance is the aravah—*the taking of a bundle of willow branches.*

Dots That Need to Be Connected

Avraham the Host

TEXT 1A

Bereishit (Genesis) 18:1-4

וַיֵּרָא אֵלָיו ה' בְּאֵלֹנֵי מַמְרֵא וְהוּא יֹשֵׁב פֶּתַח הָאֹהֶל כְּחֹם הַיּוֹם:
וַיִּשָּׂא עֵינָיו וַיַּרְא וְהִנֵּה שְׁלֹשָׁה אֲנָשִׁים נִצָּבִים עָלָיו וַיַּרְא וַיָּרָץ לִקְרָאתָם
מִפֶּתַח הָאֹהֶל וַיִּשְׁתַּחוּ אָרְצָה:
וַיֹּאמַר אֲדֹנָי אִם נָא מָצָאתִי חֵן בְּעֵינֶיךָ אַל נָא תַעֲבֹר מֵעַל עַבְדֶּךָ:
יֻקַּח נָא מְעַט מַיִם וְרַחֲצוּ רַגְלֵיכֶם וְהִשָּׁעֲנוּ תַּחַת הָעֵץ:

Now G-d appeared to him in the plains of Mamre, and he was sitting at the entrance of the tent when the day was hot.

And he lifted his eyes and saw, and behold, three men were standing beside him, and he saw and he ran toward them from the entrance of the tent, and he prostrated himself to the ground.

And he said, "My lords, if only I have found favor in your eyes, please do not pass on from beside your servant.

Please let a little water be taken, and bathe your feet, and recline under the tree.

A Tree for a Tree

TEXT 1B

Midrash Bereishit Rabah, 48:10

Bereishit Rabah

An early rabbinic commentary on the Book of Genesis. This Midrash bears the name of Rabbi Oshiya Rabah (Rabbi Oshiya "the Great"), whose teaching opens this work. This Midrash provides textual exegeses and stories, expounds upon the biblical narrative, and develops and illustrates moral principles. Produced by the sages of the Talmud in the Land of Israel, its use of Aramaic closely resembles that of the Jerusalem Talmud. It was first printed in Constantinople in 1512 together with four other Midrashic works on the other four books of the Pentateuch.

אתה אמרת והשענו תחת העץ חייך שאני פורע לבניך . . . בסוכות תשבו שבעת ימים.

You said, "Recline under the tree"—by your life, I will repay your children for this . . . as the verse states, "You shall dwell in sukkot for seven days."

Leviathan Leather

TEXT 2

Yalkut Shimoni, Iyov Remez 927

Yalkut Shimoni

A Midrash that covers the entire biblical text. Its material is collected from all over rabbinic literature, including the Babylonian and Jerusalem Talmuds and various ancient Midrashic texts. It contains several passages from Midrashim that have been lost, as well as different versions of existing Midrashim. It is unclear when and by whom this Midrash was redacted.

כל מי שמקיים מצות סוכה בעולם הזה אף הקדוש ברוך הוא מושיבו בסוכתו של לויתן לעתיד לבוא שנאמר התמלא בשכות עורו וגו'.

Whoever fulfills the mitzvah of sukkah in this world— G-d settles him in the Leviathan's sukkah in the World to Come, as the verse states, "Will you fulfill [your desire] to make a tent of his skin," etc.

The Gentiles' Complaint

TEXT 3

Talmud Tractate Avodah Zarah, 3a–b

Babylonian Talmud

A literary work of monumental proportions that draws upon the legal, spiritual, intellectual, ethical, and historical traditions of Judaism. The 37 tractates of the Babylonian Talmud contain the teachings of the Jewish sages from the period after the destruction of the Second Temple through the 5th century CE. It has served as the primary vehicle for the transmission of the Oral Law and the education of Jews over the centuries; it is the entry point for all subsequent legal, ethical, and theological Jewish scholarship.

אמרו לפניו רבונו של עולם תנה לנו מראש ונעשנה! אמר להן
הקדוש ברוך הוא שוטים שבעולם מי שטרח בערב שבת יאכל
בשבת מי שלא טרח בערב שבת מהיכן יאכל בשבת אלא אף על
פי כן מצוה קלה יש לי וסוכה שמה לכו ועשו אותה . . . ואמאי קרי
ליה מצוה קלה משום דלית ביה חסרון כיס.

מיד כל אחד [ואחד] נוטל והולך ועושה סוכה בראש גגו והקדוש
ברוך הוא מקדיר עליהם חמה בתקופת תמוז וכל אחד ואחד
מבעט בסוכתו ויוצא שנאמר ננתקה את מוסרותימו ונשליכה ממנו
עבותימו מקדיר והא אמרת אין הקדוש ברוך הוא בא בטרוניא עם
בריותיו משום דישראל נמי זימני דמשכא להו תקופת תמוז עד
חגא והוי להו צערא. והאמר רבא מצטער פטור מן הסוכה? נהי
דפטור בעוטי מי מבעטי מיד הקדוש ברוך הוא יושב ומשחק עליהן
שנאמר יושב בשמים ישחק וגו'.

The gentiles say before G-d, "Master of the Universe, give us the Torah afresh and we will perform its mitzvot." The Holy One, Blessed be He, says to them, "Fools of the world! One who takes pains on Shabbat eve will eat on Shabbat, but one who did not take pains on Shabbat eve, from where will he eat on Shabbat? But even so, I have an easy mitzvah to fulfill, and its name is sukkah; go and perform it." . . .

Now, why does G-d call the mitzvah of sukkah an easy mitzvah to fulfill? Because performing the mitzvah involves no monetary loss.

Immediately, each and every gentile will take materials and go and construct a sukkah on top of his roof. And the Holy One, Blessed be He, will set upon them the heat of the sun in the season of Tamuz, [i.e., the summer, and each and every one who is sitting in his sukkah will be unable to stand the heat,] and he will kick his sukkah and leave, as it is stated: "Let us break their bands asunder and cast away their cords from us." . . .

Immediately, the Holy One, Blessed be He sits and makes sport of those gentiles, i.e., He laughs at them, as it is stated, "He that sits in heaven makes sport, G-d has them in derision."

Commitment vs. Fulfillment

The Easiest Mitzvah

TEXT 4

Talmud Tractate Sukkah 26a

חולים ומשמשיהם: תנו רבנן חולה שאמרו לא חולה שיש בו
סכנה אלא אפילו חולה שאין בו סכנה אפילו חש בעיניו ואפילו
חש בראשו.
אמר רבי שמעון בן גמליאל פעם אחת חשתי בעיני בקיסרי והתיר
רבי יוסי בריבי לישן אני ומשמשי חוץ לסוכה. רב שרא לרב אחא
ברדלא למגנא בכילתא בסוכה משום בקי. רבא שרא ליה לרבי
אחא בר אדא למגנא בר ממטללתא משום סירחא דגרגישתא. רבא
לטעמיה דאמר רבא מצטער פטור מן הסוכה.

*[The Talmud quotes the Mishnah:] The ill and their
caretakers are exempt from the mitzvah of sukkah.
The Sages taught in a Beraita: The ill person that they
said is exempt from sukkah is not only an ill person
whose condition is critical, but even an ill person whose
condition is not critical, and even one who feels pain in
his eyes, and even one who feels pain in his head.*

*Rabban Shimon ben Gamliel said: One time I felt
pain in my eyes in Caesarea, and the esteemed Rabbi
Yosei ben Chalafta permitted me and my attendant*

to sleep outside the sukkah. [The Talmud relates a similar tale]: Rav permitted Rav Acha Bardela to sleep beneath a canopy in the sukkah due to the biting flies. Rava permitted Rabbi Acha bar Adda to sleep outside the sukkah due to the foul odor of the earth floor of the sukkah. [The Talmud comments:] Rava conforms to his line of reasoning, as Rava said: One who suffers in the sukkah is exempt from the mitzvah of sukkah.

Two Types of Love

TEXT 5

Rabbi Menachem Mendel Schneerson of Lubavitch, the Tzemach Tzedek, Biurei Zohar, Pekudei p. 310

Rabbi Menachem Mendel Schneersohn of Lubavitch
(*Tzemach Tzedek*)
1789–1866

Chasidic rebbe and noted author. The *Tzemach Tzedek* was the third leader of the Chabad Chasidic movement and a noted authority on Jewish law. His numerous works include halachic responsa, Chasidic discourses, and kabbalistic writings. Active in the communal affairs of Russian Jewry, he worked to alleviate the plight of the cantonists, Jewish children kidnapped to serve in the Czar's army. He passed away in Lubavitch, leaving seven sons and two daughters.

ולכאורה קשה: למה יבעטו בסוכה יצאו בדין מן הסוכה הלא מצטער פטור מן הסוכה?

אך הוא מטעם שעיקר עשייתם הוא רק לגרמיה ואפילו אם עושים לפעם לפעם מצוה הוא רק להתראות שהם עושים ולכן יבעטו שלא נשלמה רצונם אבל בישראל הוא רק לעשות רצון קונם ולכן אם הקדוש ברוך הוא רוצה שיעשה על ידי מה טוב ובאם שאינו רוצה כמו המצטער שפטור מן השינה ואין הקדוש ברוך הוא רוצה שתשלם מצוה והרצון על ידי גם כן סובלים ומסכימים לרצונו בתכלית הביטול יהיה איך שיהיה . . .

כי יש ב' בחינות אהבה היינו בחינה א' שאדם אוהב לחבירו וממלא רצונו בכל מה דאפשר אך כוונתו שיהא הוא האוהב והוא העושה וממלא רצונו וזה בחינות לגרמיה עדיין. ובחינה ב' הוא שאוהב את חבירו בתכלית ורוצה שיתמלא רצונו מכל הצדדים ואף גם שלא יהיה הוא בזה משפיע הטובה למילוי רצונו מכל מקום רוצה בזה מאד וזהו בחינת אהבה האמיתית מכל צד, ודי למבין.

The matter is puzzling: Why would they kick the sukkah, rather than simply exit it, being that "one who suffers [in the sukkah] is exempt from performing the mitzvah of sukkah?"

The answer is that they perform this mitzvah in a way that is founded on their own self-interest. When the average person performs a mitzvah, it is to show that he is performing it. Thus, he will kick the sukkah when it does not fulfill his personal goal.

But a Jew ought to perform a mitzvah purely to fulfill G-d's will. Thus, if G-d desires for the mitzvah to be performed through him, he is happy. But even if G-d evidently does not wish for the mitzvah to be fulfilled by him—such as one who suffers in it and is therefore not obligated to sleep in the sukkah—he likewise accepts it humbly as G-d's will, whatever the case may be.

For there are two types of love. The first is that of one who loves his friend and wishes to fulfill that friend's every desire, but the true motive is the satisfaction of being a good friend and of providing for him. *Ulti-mately, this is a selfish motive. The second type is that of one who is genuinely concerned with his friend's happiness; even if he doesn't get to be the one providing it, he is still very happy that his friend's desire has been fulfilled. This is true and complete love.*

Being for G-d

TEXT 6A

Mishlei (Proverbs) 3:6

בְּכָל דְּרָכֶיךָ דָעֵהוּ וְהוּא יְיַשֵּׁר אֹרְחֹתֶיךָ:

Know Him in all your ways, and He will direct your paths.

TEXT 6B

The Lubavitcher Rebbe, Likutei Sichot, vol. 2, p. 418

Rabbi Menachem Mendel Schneerson
1902–1994
The towering Jewish leader of the 20th century, known as "the Lubavitcher Rebbe," or simply as "the Rebbe." Born in southern Ukraine, the Rebbe escaped Nazi-occupied Europe, arriving in the U.S. in June 1941. The Rebbe inspired and guided the revival of traditional Judaism after the European devastation, impacting virtually every Jewish community the world over. The Rebbe often emphasized that the performance of just one additional good deed could usher in the era of Mashiach. The Rebbe's scholarly talks and writings have been printed in more than 200 volumes.

מען מאנט ביי א אידן עס זאל זיין בכל דרכיך דעהו, אז אלע זיינע ענינים זאלן זיין פארבונדן מיטן אויבערשטן. ניט נאר בשעת לימוד התורה ועבודת התפלה זאל ער דינען דעם אויבערשטן, נאר אפילו בשעת ער האט גאר צו טאן מיט עובדין דחול, דארף ער די עובדין דחול גופא פארבינדן מיטן אויבערשטן.

A Jew ought to serve G-d in the way described in the verse, "Know Him in all your ways," namely, that everything he or she does is associated with G-d. One should not only serve G-d while learning Torah or praying; rather, even when one is occupied with mundane matters, those very mundane matters should be associated with G-d.

Living for One Purpose

TEXT 7A

Mishnah, Kidushin 4:14

רבי שמעון בן אלעזר . . . אני נבראתי לשמש את קוני.

Rabbi Shimon ben Elazar says . . . I was created to serve the One who formed me.

TEXT 7B

Ibid., Manuscript Version

אני לא נבראתי אלא לשמש את קוני.

I was not created for any purpose other than serving my Creator.

Mishnah

The first authoritative work of Jewish law that was codified in writing. The Mishnah contains the oral traditions that were passed down from teacher to student; it supplements, clarifies, and systematizes the commandments of the Torah. Due to the continual persecution of the Jewish people, it became increasingly difficult to guarantee that these traditions would not be forgotten. Rabbi Yehudah Hanasi therefore redacted the Mishnah at the end of the second century. It serves as the foundation for the Talmud.

Sukkahs as a Prototype

TEXT 8

Shulchan Aruch, Orach Chayim, 639:1

Rabbi Yosef Caro
(Maran, *Beit Yosef*)
1488–1575

Halachic authority and author.
Rabbi Caro was born in Spain,
but was forced to flee during
the expulsion in 1492 and
eventually settled in Safed,
Israel. He authored many
works including the *Beit Yosef*,
Kesef Mishneh, and a mystical
work, *Magid Meisharim*.
Rabbi Caro's magnum opus,
the Shulchan Aruch (Code
of Jewish Law), has been
universally accepted as the
basis for modern Jewish law.

כיצד מצות ישיבה בסוכה שיהיה אוכל ושותה (וישן ומטייל) ודר
בסוכה כל שבעת הימים בין ביום ובין בלילה כדרך שהוא דר בביתו
בשאר ימות השנה וכל שבעת ימים עושה אדם את ביתו עראי ואת
סוכתו קבע כיצד כלים הנאים ומצעות הנאות בסוכה וכלי שתיה
כגון אשישות וכוסות בסוכה.

*How is the mitzvah of sukkah fulfilled? By eating
and drinking and sleeping and relaxing and living in
the sukkah for all seven days of the holiday, day and
night, just as one lives inside his home during the rest of
the year. For all seven days of the holiday, one should
make his home his secondary residence and his sukkah
his primary residence. How so? One should bring their
nice dishes and nice bedding and cups and goblets into
the sukkah.*

TEXT 9

The Rebbe, Reshimot booklet 62, p. 21

ולכן נקראת גם כן "מצוה קלה"—כיון שענינה שאין משנה מאומה
מארחו והנהגותיו, ואדרבה, החיוב הוא שיתנהג כהנהגתו כל השנה
כולה, אלא שיעשה זאת בסוכה.

*Therefore, [sukkah] is called an "easy mitzvah"—for
it doesn't change anything in one's routine. To the
contrary, the obligation is to act as one would all year
long, but to do so inside the sukkah.*

TEXT 10A

The Lubavitcher Rebbe, Likutei Sichot, vol. 2, p. 418

און דעם כוח און שטאַרקייט אויף דעם נעמט מען פון דער מצות
סוכה. ביי דער מצוה פון סוכה איז דאָך אפילו ווען ער שלאָפט
אין דער סוכה איז ער מקיים א מצוה פון דעם אויבערשטן, און
אפילו ווען ער געפינט זיך גאָר ניט אין סוכה, אויך דעמאָלט איז ער
פארבונדן מיט דער מצוה, און פון דעם דארף ער נעמען כוח און
שטאַרקייט אויף א גאַנץ יאָר, אז אין אלע זיינע ענינים זאל ער זיין
משועבד צו אלקות.

*The power and strength to ["Know G-d in all your
ways,] stems from the mitzvah of sukkah. The sukkah
is unique in that even when a person sleeps in it, he
fulfills a commandment of G-d. During Sukkot, even*

when one is not actually in the sukkah, he is connected to the mitzvah. From this, one ought to draw strength and power for the entire year to live in a way that everything he does is connected to G-dliness.

Love What You do, Never Work a Day in Your Life

TEXT 10B

Ibid.

די גמרא רופט אן די מצות סוכה מיטן נאמען מצוה קלה. וואָרום בשעת א איד שטעלט זיך אַוועק מיט א תוקף, זאָל זיין וואָס עס וועט זיין, איך בין אן עבד למלך מלכי המלכים הקדוש ברוך הוא, דעמאָלט איז אים לייכט דורכצופירן, אז אויך זיינע צרכים הגשמיים זאָלן זיין כדבעי למהוי, און ער מאַכט אויך בתחתונים א דירה לו יתברך.

The Talmud refers to sukkah as an "easy mitzvah." When a Jew firmly resolves that, "Come what may, I am a servant of the King, King of Kings, the Holy One Blessed be He," it does, in fact become quite easy; a person's physical matters can be as they should, and he is able to make that worldly, material space into something G-dly.

The Ultimate Connection

Above and Beyond the Call of Duty

TEXT 11

The Rebbe, Reshimot booklet 62 p. 11

שלכן ניתנה מצות סוכה דוקא בשכר "והשענו תחת העץ", שהיה בזה ענין של הידור מצוה, כי, עיקר מצות הכנסת אורחים הוא אכילה שתיה לויה ואילו "והשענו תחת העץ" הוא ענין של תוספת הידור, שזהו מורה על התמסרותו ביותר לקיים רצון המצוה (עילוי היותר אפשרי).

The mitzvah of sukkah serves as a reward for Abra-ham's inviting his guests to "recline under the tree" because that invitation represented beautifying *the mitzvah [of* hachnasat orachim*]. The basic mitzvah of* hachnasat orachim *consists of* eshel: *providing food, drink, and escorting the guest on his way. By contrast, inviting guests to "recline under the tree" goes above and beyond the call of duty, which demonstrates Abra-ham's utmost dedication to fulfilling G-d's will to the best of his ability.*

The Leviathan Connection

TEXT 12A

Bereishit (Genesis) 29:34

> וַתַּהַר עוֹד וַתֵּלֶד בֵּן וַתֹּאמֶר עַתָּה הַפַּעַם יִלָּוֶה אִישִׁי אֵלַי כִּי יָלַדְתִּי לוֹ
> שְׁלֹשָׁה בָנִים עַל כֵּן קָרָא שְׁמוֹ לֵוִי:

And she conceived again and bore a son, and she said, "Now this time my husband will be attached to me, for I have borne him three sons"; therefore, He named him Levi.

TEXT 12B

Rabbi Shneur Zalman of Liadi, Likutei Torah, Shemini 18b

Rabbi Shneur Zalman of Liadi
(Alter Rebbe)
1745–1812
Chasidic rebbe, halachic authority, and founder of the Chabad movement. The Alter Rebbe was born in Liozna, Belarus, and was among the principal students of the Magid of Mezeritch. His numerous works include the *Tanya*, an early classic containing the fundamentals of Chabad Chasidism, and *Shulchan Aruch HaRav*, an expanded and reworked code of Jewish law.

> וישנם בכל דור ודור שהם צדיקים שבסתר כו' והם המחברים
> העולמות לאין סוף ברוך הוא (ועל דרך שאמרו דוד היה מחבר
> תורה שלמעלה בהקדוש ברוך הוא) וזהו ענין לויתן שהוא לשון
> התחברות כמו הפעם ילוה אישי אלי כו'.

In every generation there are hidden tzaddikim . . . who connect the worlds to the Divine Light (similar to King David who "would connect the supernal Torah to G-d") which is the idea of the Leviathan, whose name connotes attachment, as in, "This time my husband will be attached to me, etc."

TEXT 13

Ibid. p. 13

ולעתיד לבוא, שאז יהיה שכר המצות, שכר מצוה מצוה, בגילוי -
הנה אז תהיה סוכת עורו של לויתן.

"לויתן" - לשון חבור וצותא". וגם, "כל שבים טהור", ואין שייך שם
מציאות הטומאה כלל, ועד שדגים נמצאים תמיד במקום חיותם.

וזהו שבזכות מצות סוכה (שבה נרמזו כל עניני המצוות, כנ"ל
באורכה) יזכו לעתיד לבוא לסוכת עורו של לויתן - **לפי שאז**
(לעתיד לבוא) יהיו כל מקיימי תורה ומצות עתה - **בבחינה זו**
(ד"לויתן", חבור וצותא, שלילת מציאות הטומאה לגמרי, והדביקות
במקום חיותם) **בגילוי, שזהו עיקר שכר המצות,** שכר מצוה מצוה,
ההתעצמות עם המצוה.

The sukkah made of the Leviathan's skin will be when Mashiach comes, when the reward for mitzvot— and "the reward for a mitzvah is a mitzvah"—will be revealed.

"Livyatan" [Leviathan] connotes connection and attachment. Furthermore, the Mishnah states, "Everything in the sea is pure"; the whole concept of impurity is absent from the sea, to the point that "fish are constantly in their life-source."

This is why the Jewish people will merit to enter the sukkah made of the Leviathan's skin as reward for the mitzvah of sukkah (which alludes to general concept of all mitzvot): When Moshiach comes, we, who observe the Torah and mitzvot in the current era, will all be at this level (of "Leviathan," of absolute connection with G-d, of the absence of impurity, and connection with our life-source) in a revealed fashion, which is the main reward for mitzvot.

TEXT 14

Rabbi Moshe Isserles, Rama, Orach Chaim 667:1

Rabbi Moshe Isserlis
(Rama)
1525–1572
Halachist. Rama served as rabbi in Krakow, Poland, and is considered the definitive authority on Jewish law among Ashkenazic Jewry. Rama authored glosses (known as the *Mapah*) on the Shulchan Aruch and *Darchei Moshe*, a commentary on the halachic compendium *Arbaah Turim*.

ויש שנהגו כשהיו יוצאים מן הסוכה היו אומרים יהי רצון שנזכה לישב בסוכה של לויתן.

Some have had the custom to recite, upon leaving the sukkah, "May it be Your Will that we merit to sit in the Sukkah of the Leviathan."

THE ROHR
Jewish Learning Institute

822 Eastern Parkway, Brooklyn, New York 11213

CHAIRMAN
Rabbi Moshe Kotlarsky
Lubavitch World Headquarters, New York

PRINCIPAL BENEFACTOR
Mr. George Rohr
New York, NY

EXECUTIVE DIRECTOR
Rabbi Efraim Mintz

ADMINISTRATOR
Rabbi Dubi Rabinowitz

EXECUTIVE COMMITTEE
Rabbi Chaim Block
S. Antonio, TX

Rabbi Hesh Epstein
Columbia, SC

Rabbi Ronnie Fine
Montreal, Quebec

Rabbi Yosef Gansburg
Toronto, Ontario

Rabbi Shmuel Kaplan
Potomac, MD

Rabbi Yisrael Rice
S. Rafael, CA

Rabbi Avrohom Sternberg
New London, CT

TORAH STUDIES

CHAIRMAN
Rabbi Yosef Gansburg
Toronto, Ontario

MANAGING EDITOR
Rabbi Ahrele Loschak
Brooklyn, NY

ADMINISTRATOR
Rabbi Levi Kaplan
Brooklyn, NY

FOUNDING DIRECTOR
Rabbi Meir Hecht
Chicago, IL

STEERING COMMITTEE
Rabbi Levi Fogelman
Natick, MA

Rabbi Yaakov Halperin
Allentown, PA

Rabbi Nechemiah Schusterman
Peabody, MA

Rabbi Ari Sollish
Atlanta, GA

CONTENT EDITORS
Rabbi Shneur Broh
Brooklyn, NY

Rabbi Zalman Ives
Brooklyn, NY

Rabbi Sholom Ber Notik
Brooklyn, NY

Shmuel Loebenstein
Brooklyn, NY

Rabbi Boruch Werdiger
Jerusalem, Israel

MARKETING AND PR
Rabbi Zalman M. Abraham
Sheva Rivkin

TEXTBOOK DESIGN
Shternie Morozow
Rabbi Zalman Korf

COPYEDITING
Mr. Michael Barnett
Bel Air, MD

POWERPOINT DESIGN
Mrs. Bunie Chazan
Manchester, England

Rabbi Cheski Edelman
Olympia, WA

PRODUCTION
Rabbi Mendel Sirota
Brooklyn, NY

An affiliate of
Merkos L'Inyonei Chinuch
The Educational Arm of the Worldwide
Chabad Lubavitch Movement

JEWISH LEARNING INSTITUTE

THE JEWISH LEARNING MULTIPLEX
Brought to you by the Rohr Jewish Learning Institute

In fulfillment of the mandate of the Lubavitcher Rebbe, of blessed memory,
whose leadership guides every step of our work,
the mission of the Rohr Jewish Learning Institute is to transform
Jewish life and the greater community through the study of Torah,
connecting each Jew to our shared heritage of Jewish learning.

While our flagship program remains the cornerstone of our organization,
JLI is proud to feature additional divisions catering to specific populations,
in order to meet a wide array of educational needs.

THE ROHR JEWISH LEARNING INSTITUTE,
a subsidiary of *Merkos L'Inyonei Chinuch*,
is the adult education arm of the Chabad-Lubavitch Movement.